BUSHCRAFT

Learn the Art of Wilderness Survival & Rediscover Your Connection to Nature | Fire Building, Water Purification, First Aid, Shelter Building & Wild Edible Plants

Jack Arrow

Jack Arrow © Copyright 2023 - All rights reserved.

The content contained within this book may not be reproduced, duplicated or transmitted without direct written permission from the author or the publisher.

Under no circumstances will any blame or legal responsibility be held against the publisher, or author, for any damages, reparation, or monetary loss due to the information contained within this book. Either directly or indirectly.

Legal Notice:

This book is copyright protected. This book is only for personal use. You cannot amend, distribute, sell, use, quote or paraphrase any part, or the content within this book, without the consent of the author or publisher.

Disclaimer Notice:

Please note the information contained within this document is for educational and entertainment purposes only. All effort has been executed to present accurate, up to date, and reliable, complete information. No warranties of any kind are declared or implied. Readers acknowledge that the author is not engaging in the rendering of legal, financial, medical or professional advice. The content within this book has been derived from various sources. Please consult a licensed professional before attempting any techniques outlined in this book.

By reading this document, the reader agrees that under no circumstances is the author responsible for any losses, direct or indirect, which are incurred as a result of the use of information contained within this document, including, but not limited to, — errors, omissions, or inaccuracies.

TABLE OF CONTENTS

PART 1: INTRODUCTION TO BUSHCRAFT 11

CHAPTER 1: WHAT IS BUSHCRAFT? 11
- The benefits of learning bushcraft skills 11
- Basic principles of bushcraft 13
- The ethics of bushcraft 14
  - Respect for nature 14
  - Respect for animals 14
  - Knowledge sharing 15

CHAPTER 2: SHELTER-BUILDING 16
- The importance of shelter in survival situations 16
- Choosing a location for your shelter 16
- Types of shelters 17
  - Lean to shelter 17
  - Frame shelter 17
  - Tent shelter 18
  - Hut shelter 19
  - Suspended shelter 20
  - Debris shelter 20
- Materials for shelter-building 21
- How to build a shelter step-by-step 22

PART 2: FIRE - WATER- FOOD GUIDE 24

CHAPTER 1: FIRE-STARTING 24
- The importance of fire in survival situations 24
- Types of fire 26
  - Fire Dakota Hole 28
  - Hut fire 29
  - Swedish torch 30

Teepee fire 30

Wheel or star fire 31

Hunter's fire 32

Screen fire 32

Trench fire 32

Pit fire or Polynesian 32

Key fire 33

Fire-starting tools 33

Matches 33

Lighter 33

Firesteel 33

Piston Fire Starter 35

Friction-based fire-starting methods 35

Lighting the fire with the bow 35

Hand-to-hand ignition technique 36

Fire piston ignition method 37

Other primitive fire-starting methods 37

Magnifying glass and sun rays 37

Flint 38

Making fire with the belt method 38

Safety rules for lighting a fire 39

Where to find fuel to make fire 39

CHAPTER 2: WATER PROCUREMENT AND PURIFICATION 40

The importance of water in survival situations 40

Sources of water in the wilderness 41

Water purification methods 42

Purify water with the classic method: boiling 42

Boil water with hot rocks 42

The distillation of water 43

How to build a water filter 44

How to collect and store water 44

Collect rainwater 44

How to collect water in a swamp 44

Collect plant transpiration 45

Collect water from snow and ice...45

CHAPTER 3: FOOD PROCUREMENT..47

The importance of food in survival situations 47

Edible plants and fruits..47

Hunting and trapping game 51

Bow and Arrow Hunting 51

Hunting with snares or snaring...51

Crossbow Hunting 52

Fishing and gathering seafood 52

Preparation and cooking methods...54

PART 3: TRAPPING 101 56

CHAPTER 1: TRAPPING 56

The importance of trapping in bushcraft 56

Types of traps 56

Bow Trap 56

Box trap 57

Drop trap 58

Conibear trap..58

Setting traps for small game 60

Setting traps for larger game 60

Ethical considerations in trapping 61

PART 4: NAVIGATION AND KNOTS 63

CHAPTER 1: NAVIGATION 63

The importance of navigation in the wilderness..63

Navigation tools..63

Topographic map..63

Compass 64

- Altimeter 64
- GPS 64
- Wristwatch 65

How to read a map and use a compass **66**
- How to use the compass 67

Natural navigation methods **68**
- Orientation with the sun 68
- Orientation with the moon 68
- Orient yourself with the stars 69
- How to orient yourself with plants 69

How to stay on course and avoid getting lost **70**

CHAPTER 2: KNOT-TYING AND ROPE WORK **72**

The importance of rope in bushcraft **72**

Types of rope and cordage **72**
- Paracord 72
- Jute twine 73
- The sisal rope 73
- Propylene rope 74
- Kevlar rope 74
- White line rope 75

Basic knots **76**
- Slipped Overhand knot 76
- Timber Hitch Knot 77
- Half Hitch Knot 77

Advanced knots **78**
- Double Fisherman's Knot 78
- Clove Hitch Knot 79
- The Carrick Knot 80
- Prusik's knot 81
- The bowline knot 82

How to make rope from natural materials 83

PART 5: CAMP CRAFT AND FIRST AID CRASH COURSE 85

CHAPTER 1: TOOLMAKING AND CAMP CRAFTS 85

The importance of tools in bushcraft 85

Basic toolmaking 86

- The basics 86
- Ax 86
- Bags and backpacks 87
- Look for water to make drinkable 87
- Knife 88
- Types of Knife Steel 89
- Benchmade Bushcrafter Knife 89
- Condor Knife & Tool Bushlore 90
- Buck Knives Bu853brs 90
- Spyderco G-10 Bushcraft Knife 91
- Tops Brothers of Bushcraft 91
- Morakniv Carbon Black Tactical Bushcraft Knife 92
- Ontario Sk-5 Blackbird 92
- Helle Utvaer 93
- Zippo lighter and windproof matches 93
- Water bottle with mess tin 94
- Paracord 94
- Head Torch 95
- Waterproof poncho 95
- Sleeping bag 95
- Tarp or Tent 95
- Single-person tents 96
- Tarp Bushcraft 96
- Bushcraft clothing, shirts and trousers 97

Advanced toolmaking (woodworking, metalworking, etc.) 97
Tools Make fires in the woods 97
The stack the fire 98
Fire Dakota Hole 98
Swedish torch 98
Woodworking tools.. 98

Camp crafts (baskets, mats, containers, etc.) 100
Baskets 100
Mats 100
Containers 101

How to maintain and care for your tools... 101

CHAPTER 2: FIRST AID AND MEDICAL EMERGENCIES 103

The importance of first aid in the wilderness 103
Key word: prevention is better than cure 103
First aid: why is it so important? 104

Basic first aid skills 104
The accident and the examination of the injured... 104
State of consciousness 105
Respiratory function... 105
Heart function 105
Fractures and bleeding: how to recognize them and what to do 106
Fractures 106
Splinting 106
How to remove a splinter of glass 107
How to remove a wood splinter.. 107
Bleeding and wounds 107
Waiting for help 107

Common medical emergencies 108
Hypothermia... 108
Treatment of hypothermia 108

Dehydration 109

The most common symptoms 109

Water and supplements always in the backpack 110

How to create a first aid kit 110

How to prepare for medical emergencies in the wilderness 111

Personal emergency supplies 111

Read a first aid manual carefully 112

PART 6: WILDERNESS SURVIVALIST MINDSET 113

CHAPTER 1: SURVIVAL PSYCHOLOGY AND MINDSET 113

The importance of a positive mindset in survival situations 113

How to stay calm and focused in stressful situations 113

How to deal with fear and anxiety 115

How to prepare mentally for survival situations 116

The role of mindfulness and meditation in bushcraft 116

PART 7: WEATHER AND SURVIVALISM SKILLS 118

CHAPTER 1: WEATHER AND CLIMATE 118

The importance of understanding weather and climate in bushcraft 118

Basic meteorology 118

Reading weather patterns 120

How to prepare for different weather conditions 122

How to deal with the rain 123

Dealing with extreme weather conditions 123

How to deal with blizzards 123

Hurricanes 124

Floods 125

CHAPTER 2: NATURALIST SKILLS AND ENVIRONMENTAL AWARENESS 126

The importance of understanding and appreciating nature in bushcraft 126

Basic ecology 126

Wildlife identification and behavior 128

Wolf 129

Bear 130

Wild boars...131

Ticks...131

Venomous snakes 132

Ethical considerations in bushcraft..**133**

How to develop a connection to the natural **133**

PART 8: COMPLETE LIST OF MOST IMPORTANT EQUIPMENTS AND TOOLS 136

Bushcraft backpacks and bags **136**

Bushcraft clothing, shirts and trousers 136

Survival equipment and accessories...137

Water bag for bushcraft...137

Tarp: the waterproof bushcraft tarp 138

Bushcraft hammock...139

Water bottle with mess tin 140

Head Torch 140

Sleeping bag..141

PART 1: INTRODUCTION TO BUSHCRAFT

Chapter 1: What is bushcraft?

Bushcraft is the practice that teaches survival methods in wooded or natural areas, using only the resources available in nature.

Without any artificial help then. No electronic or mechanical means, no tools you usually use in everyday life. Only you, in the wilderness.

Bushcraft is among the latest trends in total and wild nature experiences born to reconnect with nature, recovering the ancient knowledge of the forest now forgotten.

It's called Bushcraft and it's the term that now includes more and more experiences in nature made of survival, minimal camping, trekking and hiking.

The word bushcraft indicates all survival techniques, which include the ability to light a fire, being able to follow the tracks of animals, being able to build a shelter, using a knife and ax effectively, recognizing edible plants and herbs, making tools in wood, knowing how to build containers using natural materials and knowing how to make ropes.

The benefits of learning bushcraft skills

Building a shelter of leaves and branches, finding water, lighting a fire yourself to warm up or cook, orienting yourself, recognizing edible plants are all experiences that reconnect with nature, but which could be defined as extreme by those who are not used to this minimal mode.

The philosophy of this technique in general is to recover all that ancient knowledge well known to our ancestors but which we have almost completely lost due to technological progress.

The need to reconnect with Nature and fill it up to regain the well-being that only total immersion in the wild environment can give is increasingly urgent. Rich and fulfilling and even wild nature experiences are not only important for spending free time, but as a real cure for body and mind.

Most people live a hectic life and today there are more and more adults and children alienated and affected by the so-called Nature Deficit Disorder or the lack of direct relationship with nature.

Bushcraft will teach you to trust in your abilities, to listen and observe nature in a whole new way, developing your perceptive, sensory and empathetic skills.

Furthermore, bushcraft is also a sharing experience, in which connections are created with oneself, with nature and also with others. Indeed, during these experiences it is discovered that the forest is not hostile but offers opportunities for survival.

Let's see in more detail what are the beneficial effects of bushcraft:
- Being in nature improves the quality of life.
- Being outdoors radically changes the physical expression of stress in our body.
- A decrease in heart rate and cortisol levels was also detected in people who spend more time in contact with nature, as well as a lower level of stress and greater job satisfaction in people who, despite working in the office, are able to see green areas from the window.
- Nature is the most powerful of stress relievers. Furthermore, nature reduces stress levels and can have positive effects on physical and mental well-being, such as the ability to concentrate and mood.
- Nature works like a great antidepressant. Staying outdoors by combining this situation with exercise also fights depression and anxiety states. Doctors believe that nature walks may be clinically useful as a supplement to existing medical treatment in cases of severe depression. Even the presence of water has a great relaxing effect and therefore a positive effect on people suffering from anxiety.
- Living outdoors lengthens life. Researchers at the Harvard School of Public Health concluded that women who live in greener areas have a 12% lower mortality rate than those who live in a greener downtown area. This research published in 2016 and which involved 108,000 US women in the period between 2000 and 2008 to analyze the risk factors associated with the main chronic diseases and among the variables the presence of green areas near their homes was examined homes. Proximity to areas with vegetation has shown a decrease in the mortality rate for kidney disease of 41%, 34% in the case of respiratory diseases and 13% in cases of cancer. To all this it must be added that a life dedicated to nature improves mental health, offers greater opportunities for social engagement, makes you do more physical activity and causes less exposure to pollution.
- Improve concentration. The natural environment has a powerful recovery effect and one of the many benefits that long walks in nature bring is to recover the ability to concentrate. Also in this case, to verify what was said, the researchers subjected groups to a test and the people who took a walk in the woods were found to be more concentrated than those who chose the walk in the city.
- Nature makes us more creative. Contact with a natural landscape such as a forest, but also a pristine beach, allows us to receive a series of sensory and visual stimuli that increase our creativity and our industriousness. Spending a day in the middle of nature has been proven to increase our ability to think and do by 50%.
- It helps to be more reflective. Meditating surrounded by greenery favors the ability to look within, to appreciate the silence that surrounds us and to feel the contact with the natural elements. It is truly a magnificent experience to experience and even a few minutes make us more reflective and serene.
- It helps us to be more confident. Getting out of the comfort zone, i.e., from the safety of our home and our daily habits, choosing to face totally new challenges that we are not used to, makes us rediscover an innate inner strength that will help us to better face any new problem we encounter during our life.

Basic principles of bushcraft

What we call Bushcraft today is at the same time a set of techniques and an attitude that once upon a time, when man lived in closer contact with nature, were widespread and common. Rediscovering this knowledge today means not only making contact with one's nature but also learning to live better the relationship with nature and solicit skills and attitudes that are also useful in everyday life.

The fundamental advice to start practicing bushcraft is to rely on the teaching of professionals and guides. There are already several associations of enthusiasts who offer courses and accompany them in their first experiences.

Furthermore, both online and in bookstores there are books, courses, blogs and videos that can be useful for learning the main techniques even if, obviously, the best way to learn is practice.

Great attention must be paid to the rules to follow both for one's own safety and for that of the environment and respect for nature. And, of course, to avoid fines.

The basic principles of bushcraft include:

- Knowledge of nature and natural resources: understand how to identify and use the plants, animals and natural resources available in the surrounding environment. For example, bushcraft enthusiasts learn to recognize edible and poisonous plants, how to identify safe sources of water, and to understand the characteristics of the terrain and surrounding vegetation. This knowledge is essential to being able to survive outdoors safely and effectively.

- Ability to Create Shelter: The ability to build shelter is one of the core skills of bushcraft. When spending time outdoors, a shelter can protect you from the elements, wind and cold, helping to maintain body heat and prevent hypothermia. There are different types of shelters that can be built in bushcraft, depending on the terrain, the season and the resources available. For example, a shelter can be built using trees, leaves, branches, moss, stones, or other natural materials. Building a shelter requires some experience and knowledge of construction techniques as well as the natural resources available. However, with practice and experience, building a shelter can become an essential skill for surviving and living outdoors comfortably and safely.

- Ability to make a fire: Knowing how to make a fire is essential for keeping heat, cooking food, and providing a source of light and protection. Knowing how to put out fires safely and responsibly is also important. The ability to start a fire in bushcraft takes practice and knowledge, but once mastered, it can become a vital skill for outdoor survival and livability.

- Ability to obtain food and water: being able to fish, hunt, gather berries, roots and herbs, and find safe sources of water. When spending time outdoors, it's important to know how to find and gather food and water to maintain your energy and hydration.

- Orientation: knowing how to orient yourself using the compass, stars, sun and other tools, as well as knowing how to build a mental map of the area. Navigation is a vital skill in bushcraft, allowing

you to navigate safely and reliably in a natural environment where modern maps and technology may not be available or usable.
- Survival skills: know first aid techniques, know how to deal with emergency situations, avoid dangerous situations and remain calm and focused on stressful situations. Survival techniques require knowledge, practice and skill, but they can mean the difference between life and death in an emergency.

The ethics of bushcraft

The bushcraft ethos is based on a set of core values that aim to promote a sustainable and environmentally friendly lifestyle. These values include:

Respect for nature

Respect for nature is a fundamental ethical value in bushcraft, since enthusiasts of this discipline spend a lot of time immersed in nature and rely on it for their survival, food, water and shelter activities. Bushcraft promotes an approach based on conservation and protection of the natural environment. Respect for nature involves understanding that we are part of an interconnected ecosystem and that every action we take can have an impact on the surrounding nature. This means that it is important to minimize the impact on the natural environment, avoiding damaging the fauna, flora and the surrounding environment.

Respect for nature also implies the responsibility to leave the natural environment in a better state than the one in which it was found. This means collecting your own waste, not damaging the surrounding nature and respecting the local flora and fauna.

Respect for nature also implies an understanding of the need to protect the natural environment for future generations. This means promoting the conservation of nature, supporting biodiversity and the local ecosystem, and contributing to the reduction of the environmental impact that we men punctually never pay attention to.

Respect for animals

The discipline of bushcraft is based on using natural resources for survival, and this can involve hunting, fishing and gathering food from wild animals. However, respect for animals also involves understanding their importance within the natural ecosystem and the need to treat them with compassion and respect. There are some fundamental ethical rules that bushcraft enthusiasts should respect to ensure respect for animals during their activities. For example, they should try to hunt only what is necessary and not waste the animals they kill. Furthermore, they should do everything possible to minimize the suffering of the animals during the hunting or fishing process, for example by using humane and pain-free trapping techniques.

Furthermore, respect for animals also implies understanding their importance within the natural ecosystem and the role they play in the conservation of the natural environment. For example, some animal species are important for plant reproduction, seed dispersal and maintaining ecological balance.

Knowledge sharing

Knowledge sharing is a very important aspect in bushcraft, as it allows the knowledge acquired during the experience of life in the open air to be disseminated and preserved and to make it grow continuously. Sharing knowledge regarding survival techniques and the skills needed to live sustainably and responsibly within the natural environment is a crucial aspect of bushcraft.

Knowledge sharing in bushcraft can take place in a variety of ways, such as through participation in online communities, learning groups, training courses, exchange and mentoring activities. In this way, bushcraft enthusiasts can learn from experts in the field and from other enthusiasts, improving their skills and developing a sense of community and belonging.

Furthermore, sharing knowledge in bushcraft also promotes the preservation of local culture and traditions related to the outdoors. This aspect is particularly important in an increasingly urbanized world detached from nature, where knowledge and traditions related to outdoor life risk being lost.

Chapter 2: Shelter-Building

The importance of shelter in survival situations

Building a shelter is a very important aspect of bushcrafting, as it can mean the difference between survival and death in extreme outdoor conditions. A good shelter protects you from the wind, rain, snow and cold, allowing you to retain body heat and shelter from the elements. You don't necessarily have to build a luxury or super-equipped refuge, on the contrary, know from the outset that living in a refuge will be anything but a pleasant or comfortable experience. However, the shelter, if done correctly will allow you to survive in extreme situations.

Building a bushcraft shelter requires a good understanding of survival techniques and the natural resources found in the surrounding environment. For example, you can use branches, leaves, ferns, moss, mud, and other natural materials to build a strong, sturdy shelter. It is also important to choose a suitable location, such as a place sheltered from the wind, close to sources of water and away from potential hazards, such as fallen trees or unstable slopes.

Additionally, building a bushcraft shelter not only helps ensure survival, but also develops skills and abilities useful for the outdoors. Building a shelter requires manual skills, creativity and patience, and can help develop a greater awareness of the natural environment and available resources.

Finally, building a bushcraft shelter can also be a personally rewarding and enriching experience. Building a shelter with your own hands and using the natural resources present in the surrounding environment can increase self-esteem, self-confidence and mental resilience.

Choosing a location for your shelter

If you build a beautiful shelter but the shelter is placed in the wrong location, know that you will soon have to abandon it. There are some basic guidelines that can help you determine a good place to build. First, avoid open fields, mountain tops, deep forest or woodland. Look for a transition area between habitats. Also choose a location free of anything that could collapse on the shelter.

Choose a location that has good drainage, where water cannot pass under your shelter. Therefore, avoid areas that can flood or become treacherous in case of heavy rains.

Look for a flat area where you can build the shelter. Avoid areas where the terrain is steep or rough, as they could be dangerous.

Do not build near bodies of water, to avoid accidental water pollution. Keep the shelter away from moisture and try to avoid places infested with insects such as mosquitoes.

Avoid areas with dangerous plants and animals. Also scrape the ground to look for anything that might prevent you from using your chosen spot.

One recommendation is to find a place for shelter that is downwind and at least 4 meters away from the place where you will light the fire. The reason is simple, shelters built with natural materials can burn easily.

Look for an area where the shelter is visible from a distance, so that it can be in an emergency.

When choosing the place to build the shelter, try to disturb the surrounding natural environment as little as possible. Do not remove plants or trees, and do not dig holes or trenches.

Avoid areas where hunting is conducted or where you may encounter dangerous wild animals, or you may risk being mistaken for an animal by some unwary hunter who may even strike you.

Types of shelters

There are different types of bushcraft shelters, which can be built depending on the resources and terrain available, the climatic conditions and the weather available. Here are some of the more common ones:

Lean to shelter

The lean-to shelter is a type of shelter widely used in bushcraft, as it is relatively easy to build and offers good protection from the elements.

It consists of an "L" shaped structure, formed by a vertical post driven into the ground and a horizontal post leaning on it, inclined towards the ground. The horizontal post can be connected to a second vertical post, or to a tree, to create additional lateral protection. Branches and leaves, or waterproof blankets, can then be placed on top of the horizontal pole to create the roof.

The attached shelter is particularly suitable for mild or temperate climates, where it is not necessary to create complete protection from wind and rain. In the event of heavy rain or strong winds, an additional waterproof tarp can be added to the open side of the shelter to create an additional barrier.

The advantage of the lean-to shelter is the ease of construction and the possibility of adapting it to the available resources, using trees or rocks as support for the horizontal pole. Furthermore, being open on one side, it allows you to have a view of the surrounding nature, making it an ideal solution for those who love contact with nature.

Frame shelter

The frame shelter is a type of shelter used in bushcraft, which involves the construction of a frame structure, on which insulating and waterproof materials are placed to create the roof and walls of the shelter.

The construction of the frame shelter involves the use of two vertical poles as the main supports, to which other horizontal and diagonal poles are then connected to create the frame structure. The posts can be set in the ground or placed on trees or rocks, depending on the resources available in the surrounding area.

Once the frame structure is completed, the roofing materials are applied. These can be leaves, branches, ferns, grass, moss or other plants that offer adequate protection from water and wind.

The advantage of the frame shelter is its sturdiness and durability, thanks to the frame structure which makes it stable even in case of strong winds. Additionally, the cover can be easily replaced or upgraded, as needed.

The frame shelter is particularly suitable for cold or very humid climates, where it is necessary to have complete protection from the elements. However, it requires more time and materials to build than other types of shelters, such as the lean-to shelter.

Tent shelter

The tent shelter is a form of temporary accommodation often used in bushcraft, an activity based on the use of natural resources to survive and live in wild environments.

In particular, the tent shelter in the context of bushcraft consists in the construction of a structure with the use of one or more tents, which serve as shelter from the wind, rain and bad weather in general.

The tents used for bushcraft shelters are generally of the light and portable type, so that they can be easily transported and set up on site. There are different types of tents used according to the needs of the environment and the season, such as dome tents, tunnel tents, igloo tents, geodesic tents, etc.

Hut shelter

The hut in the context of bushcraft is a rudimentary structure built using natural materials available locally, such as wood, branches, leaves, grass and mud. It is usually built in a protected area with little exposure to the elements, such as at the foot of a hill or hill.

To build a hut, survival techniques and knowledge of the characteristics of natural materials are used. Generally, you start by building a basic structure with branches and tree trunks, in order to create a solid frame on which you can then add the other natural materials.

The hut can be covered with leaves, grass or mud to create a protective layer from wind and rain.

Suspended shelter

The suspended shelter consists of a built structure suspended in the air, usually between two trees or between two wooden pillars. The structure consists of a platform of wood or other resistant materials, on which an awning or tarpaulin is placed to protect against wind, rain and bad weather.

Building the Hanging Shelter requires special skills, as you have to climb trees or pillars to set up the structure. Also, it's important to choose strong, strong trees that are far enough apart to support the platform.

Once the platform has been fixed between the trees or pillars, the tent or tarpaulin can be set up, creating a protected and comfortable space to sleep or shelter from the elements.

Debris shelter

The debris shelter is constructed using natural materials such as branches, leaves, grass, moss, feathers, and other plant debris. The construction of the shelter requires specific skills and knowledge, as it is necessary to choose the right materials and place them strategically to create a solid and resistant shelter.

Typically, the debris shelter is built in a protected area, such as at the foot of a tree or under a rock overhang. You start by creating a frame of branches and tree trunks, which will serve as a supporting structure. Then leaves, grass and other plant debris are placed on the structure, creating a protective layer from wind and rain.

To make the shelter more comfortable, you can also add a layer of moss or feathers to insulate the floor and create a soft, warm surface to sleep on.

A debris shelter can provide good protection from the elements and cold if built correctly, however, it does not offer the same protection as a shelter built with strong materials such as wood or metal. In any case, the debris shelter can be an effective solution in emergency situations where you have no other shelter options.

Materials for shelter-building

Before building your shelter, it will be good to remember to bring basic equipment with you, such as spare clothing, gloves, hats, rain gear, emergency blankets, one or more fire starters and, above all, remember to bring you a first aid kit.

Here are some examples of materials that can be used to build a shelter in the wild:

Wood: Wood is a strong and solid natural material that can be used to build a supporting structure of the shelter. Branches, logs, sticks and even bark can be used.

Leaves: Leaves can be used to cover the roof of the shelter and provide good protection from the elements. Leaves of any type can be used, as long as they are large enough and resistant.

Grass: Grass can be used to create a soft floor inside the shelter and provide thermal insulation from the ground.

Earth: Earth can be used to create retaining walls for shelter and to seal cracks between materials.

Rocks: Rocks can be used to create a solid, weather-resistant structure, or they can be used to create a fire near your shelter.

Mud: Mud can be used to create retaining walls and to seal cracks between materials.

The choice of materials depends on the available resources and environmental conditions, and the ability to use the available materials in a creative and innovative way.

How to build a shelter step-by-step

Even if most of us don't know carpentry, we can all be able to build a shelter. Building a bushcraft shelter takes time, patience and a lot of practice. The advice is to try several times and experiment with different techniques and materials, to become more and more expert and capable.

First, you have to find the right place to build your shelter. Finding the right place to place and build your shelter can take a significant amount of time.

The best place to build the shelter must include an area where it is easy to find the resources needed to build, as we mentioned earlier. When choosing the place, remember to use the five W method: wind, widowmaker, water, wood and wildlife.

The second step is to have a plan for building your shelter. Having a set plan of what and how to build your shelter will save you time and energy. Look around and based on what you see and what you need, decide how you want to proceed, i.e., what kind of shelter you want to build, how big it should be and above all where you want to place it.

Now go on to choose the materials to build the shelter, making sure first to use materials of an insulating type. As for building, start building from the bottom first and work your way up. So, having chosen the position, start covering the ground with natural substances and materials that can bring heat inside your shelter.

If you have sleeping bags or emergency mats or blankets, place them on top of the insulating material you have chosen for the base and then build the shelter around it. The thicker and more consistent the isolation, the better you will find yourself inside the shelter. With that done, continue adding insulation material and other debris to the shelter.

Before moving on to building the walls, you need to build the shelter frame. Most of the time, shelters are built close to natural elements such as, for example, large trees or large boulders. From these starting points, build the shelter structure on the V-shaped part of the boulder or tree. For the frame, a piece of wood a little longer than your height and solid will be inserted between the boulder or tree. This way the shelter will be large enough to fit your person and small enough not to allow heat to escape.

After building the frame it's time to move on to building the walls and roof. Since the most common shelters are A-frame or sloped shelters, the roof and walls often coincide. Regardless of which type of refuge you choose to build, the rule of solidity also applies to the roof and walls, i.e., they must be as resistant as the tree or boulder where you have decided to build the foundations of your refuge.

As for the walls, to ensure that they are further insulating, start building starting from thick and long sticks that rest against the frame by about 45°é. Place branch and wooden sticks along the length of the shelter frame. The ends of the posts should stick out a maximum of an inch or two.

To make the walls more insulating, just like for the frame, take handfuls of leaves, pine or other tree needles and pile them in all the free corners of your shelter. The more leaves and debris inserted into the walls, the warmer and safer the shelter will be.

Now cover the roof. Place more branches and debris on the supporting structure to create a cover layer for the roof of the shelter. Use weatherproof material and cover the roof completely to prevent water or snow from getting inside. Once the shelter is built, do a trial run to test its strength and weather resistance.

PART 2: FIRE - WATER- FOOD GUIDE

Chapter 1: Fire-Starting

The importance of fire in survival situations

Fire is extremely important in survival situations for several reasons. First, it can be used to keep warm and keep the body warm, especially in bad weather conditions such as cold or rain. In addition, it can be used for cooking food and purifying water, which makes it easier to obtain a safe source of food and drinking water.

Fire is also an important source of light, which can be useful for navigation and for spotting danger at night. Additionally, the smoke from the fire can be used as a distress signal, to attract the attention of any rescuers.

Let's take a closer look at some of the reasons why fire is important in emergency situations. The first reason is the most obvious of all, that is, the fire will serve you to provide you with heat. Hypothermia is a serious problem that can even lead to death, and this happens not only when temperatures are too low but it can also happen when the ambient temperature is relatively high. Are you wondering how this is possible? Simple, it may happen that you have damp or wet clothes and drying them by keeping them on without being able to warm up could cause a thermal shock to your body, even quite serious. Having a fire lit will allow you both to warm up and to be able to dry your clothes quickly. In this way you will not have to use the energy produced by your body to warm up, saving you from rather unpleasant situations.

The second reason fire is important is the sterilization of water. When you are in nature, however clear the water found in streams may seem to you, it is always better to consider it as contaminated and proceed with sterilization. Even if it doesn't seem like it, water can contain bacteria, viruses, chemical agents and parasites, all elements that can be fatal if they enter our body. Simply bringing the water to a boil will kill bacteria and viruses and make the water drinkable. However, the matter of chemical pollutants is different and in this case the water should be treated using carbon filters, which can also be easily built during your camp.

Third reason why fire is useful, also obvious and obvious, and that you will need it for cooking. Fire will help you make edible some foods that are practically inedible raw. In fact, with cooking, bacteria and viruses that populate above all in game and which can also be fatal to humans will be killed. Furthermore, fire can also be used for long-term food preservation.

Fire can also be useful for tool making. For example, tools made of wood can be made harder and more solid by placing them under a heat source. This is because, with the heat, the humidity inside the wood will be removed, causing the crystallization and hardening of the sap present. Another way to use heat to get tools and make clay waterproof so you can shape it and let it harden easily.

Another reason why fire is useful for survival is its protective function. In fact, both large animals but also insects that can annoy are reluctant, not to say frightened, by the presence of smoke and flames. Mosquitoes can create serious problems for people's health if the danger of being bitten by these insects is not prevented. So, know that the strong presence of smoke serves to mask the smell and therefore the presence of a human being towards animals.

Another reason you need fire when hiking, especially if you intend to spend many nights out, is lighting. The lighting will allow you to see in the dark during the night and will also allow you to complete the work started during the day. Lighting is a factor that must never be overlooked, especially if you decide to live in contact with nature for a long period of time. Also, many animals are nocturnal and if you decide to survive with the aid of hunting, then know that you will have to hunt at night and lighting is vital in these cases.

The fire will also serve you to prepare medicines in case you should get injured or sick and you are far enough away from the first available hospital. Some medicinal plants, which you can easily find in nature, need to be heated or cooked to release their active ingredients.

The last reason why fire is essential for survival in nature is to attract help, as we said at the beginning. Very often, especially those who are beginners, do not take into consideration the usefulness of this aspect of fire. To give a practical example, so as not to find yourself in trouble with warning signs, know that three fires in a row are a warning sign that is recognized worldwide. To signal a danger, you must first build a fire in a position in full view even from above, such as on a hill, in a treeless bay or on the side of a mountain. Then from the main fire make three small fires. Smaller fires need to be stoked with a fairly large number of dry, overgrown green material. The purpose of the green vegetation is to produce so much white smoke that it is visible even at enormous distances. While the dry material, which, as we know, burns easily, serves to create large amounts of heat, useful for increasing the smoke.

Types of fire

TYPES OF CAMPFIRE

Log Cabin Fire   Tepee Fire   Star Fire   Pyramid Fire

Long Fire   Dakota Hole Fire   T Fire   Keyhole Fire

Before talking about the different types of fires, we must also talk about the materials to be used to light these fires. So, let's start with the wood. The ideal would be to find it dry and seasoned. This would favor rapid ignition in the first case and effective combustion in the second. Contenting ourselves with giving up a good combustion efficiency, however, we must pursue rapid ignition with the wood that the context has made available to us. The first trick to learn when you start dedicating yourself to lighting a fire is to exploit the internal part of the wood. In fact, rain, snow, humidity and other bad weather, find it difficult to penetrate inside the trunk therefore, if you have the care and patience to split the previously collected wood lengthwise, you will bare the inside which, with great chances are it will be completely dry. This technique of chopping wood and using the inside to light a fire is known as batoning.

Still regarding the wood to be used for the fire, it is important to remember that the wood to be used must be dry and must not contain resin or other chemical products. Wet or damp wood is difficult to light and burns badly, generating smoke and making it difficult to keep the fire going.

There are also some species of wood that are particularly suitable for lighting a fire, including:

- Silver Fir: Silver fir is a light, soft wood that burns quickly. It is a good choice for starting a fire as it ignites easily and burns quickly, generating a large amount of heat.
- Pine: Pine is a light, soft wood that burns quickly. Like silver fir, it is easy to ignite and burns rapidly, generating a large amount of heat.
- Red Cedar: Red cedar is a soft wood that burns slowly. It is a great choice for starting a fire as it burns slowly and generates a large amount of heat.

- Birch: Birch is a light, soft wood that burns quickly. It is a good choice for starting a fire because it ignites easily and burns quickly, generating a large amount of heat.

Another fundamental element to be able to light the fire is the tinder, i.e., the flammable material which will then be used precisely for lighting and keeping the fire stable.

For the bait you can use mosses, lichens, bark splinters, dry leaves, thistle-like flower hair, dry grass, graminaceous plants, wild cobs, dry dung of herbivores, plant marrow such as elderberry.

It is always advisable to store tinder in a dry place and keep a supply ready for starting a fire. Alternatively, you can also bring a cotton ball with you. If you have some alcohol or petrol, wet the tinder to start the combustion faster. Resin from pinecones and pine logs are excellent fuels, as is the resinous oil from birch.

Once a fire is lit, baits can be prepared for future ignitions, by burning parts of marrow or fibrous plants, dry wood and dung. They are left to char on the fire and then kept in a dry place.

Now let's see what the types of fires are most used in bushcraft:

Fire Dakota Hole

The Dakota Hole fire is a small campfire, designed to minimize the visibility of the flame.
Being basically a "simple" hole in the ground the creation of the Dakota Fire
does not require any tools. Or rather: if you had a small tactical shovel with you excavation operations would be much faster. But the shovel is not absolutely necessary. You can always use a simple pointed stake to help you dig.

To make this fire you need to dig two holes in the earth. A main one that will act as a brazier and a secondary, much smaller one that will act as an air intake. The two holes will have to be joined by an air passage tunnel. In this way it will be possible to create a comfortable fire for cooking which will also offer a discreet source of heat, with a very low visual impact.

So, the first step in building a Dakota hole fire is to dig a deep hole. the Marines speak of two or three feet deep and about 1.5 feet wide and here we immediately encounter the first surprise with respect to the general idea of the Dakota fire hole that many improvised people have who have never faced the practice of this technique. In fact, many inexperienced people have made holes about half as deep as the one recommended by the marines.

This involves the basic error that the fire does not stay completely below the ground line and this means that it is taking in much more air than it should: the fire will burn much more fuel than a well done Dakota Fire.

An excellent rule to keep in mind is simply that the bigger the fire you want to build, the deeper and wider the hole must be. Personally, I would say that the Dakota hole it should be large enough to comfortably accommodate a normal fire without having to fight too much to break branches that don't fit in the hole.

The second step consists in how and in which direction to dig the second hole. The second hole should be made about 30 centimeters away from the first. The hole will be smaller and clearly you don't need a parallel and deep hole as the first one, but it will go down diagonally, to the base of the first hole.

The purpose of this tunnel is obviously to bring air to the base of the fire located in the first one.

But in which direction should the tunnel be dug? Be careful not to dig the connecting tunnel in a random direction. The aim is obviously to optimize the flow of air that receives the fire and that is why the tunnel must be dug in favor of the wind so that it is channeled correctly towards the embers. A good trick to know where the wind is blowing from even if it is so light that you can hardly feel it is to moisten your fingertip and expose it to the air; we will immediately feel one part of the finger colder than the other. Imagine the tip of your finger as if it were fire and the direction in which you feel the cold finger as the direction in which to dig the second grave.

Once this is done you will have a forced entry route for the air since the heat and flames spread from the larger hole and this will not allow oxygen to enter from above. By the way, this secondary hole in the Dakota Hole will allow you to blow oxygen into the fire without running the risk of burning your face by blowing into the main fire.

The third step is to widen the tunnel. Once you've dug the tunnel and reached the main fire, you'll find that you've dug a tunnel, roughly, as wide as your arm.

From now on you will have to focus on widening, working both sides, until the tunnel is at least twice as wide as your arm.

Remember that the bigger the tunnel, the more oxygen can enter, and this means having a fire that always has oxygen to burn and therefore does not go out easily.

Once the tunnel is completed the last step is to light the fire. It obviously does as we have always done with a traditional fire. Maybe a wooden platform will help in the first few moments before the fire eventually turns it into a layer of smoldering embers. Remember to use dead dry materials and light the fire as if you were normally on the surface.

It is of course possible to cook on the Dakota fire. Just have the foresight to put thick green branches on top of the primary hole or block them on the side of the walls. Green materials will not burn fast and will prevent your pots from falling into the fire.

Hut fire

Another method for lighting a fire is with the gable positioning. With this system, designed to allow easy ignition of the hearth and continuity of combustion, is not necessary to give continuous power supply. Here are the steps to follow to create a hut fire:

Choose a suitable place for building fire. Look for a place that is open and well away from trees and shrubs. The soil should be dry and there should be no dry vegetation around the place.

Prepare the ground. Remove all organic material such as leaves, grass and branches from the ground where you intend to light the fire. Dig the ground a bit until you reach a level of compacted earth.

Collect the wood. Gather dry and dead wood of various sizes, including twigs, branches, and larger logs. Make sure there is enough wood to keep the fire going.

Now go build the fire. Take a piece of dry wood and use it to make a hole in the ground. Place the dry twigs and leaves inside. Then, on top of the twigs, place small branches. Next, add the larger branches arranged in a gable on top of the smaller branches.

Light the fire using a match or lighter. Keep enough air and gently fan the flames until the fire is well lit. Make sure you don't add too much wood at once, so you don't smother the fire.

Swedish torch

The Swedish torch is the favorite solution of the "Swedish" lumberjacks, mainly used for cooking in the open air. It can be created with an ax or more easily with a chainsaw, it allows you to create a flame inside a log, making it easier to place pots for cooking or boiling.

To make the Swedish torch, all you need is a hacksaw or a switchblade and a piece of tree trunk, possibly resinous (pine, fir, larch, birch), about thirty centimeters in diameter and fifty centimeters in height.

Now let's see in detail the simple steps necessary to create this tool. Therefore, just cross-saw the tree trunk, thus dividing it into four equal parts and then insert shavings, small sticks or lichens into the slots. Then the fire is lit on at least two arms of the cross, adding sticks as the fire revives and continuing with the additions until the quarter logs have caught fire.

At this point the Swedish torch is ready to be used as a stove and, once the food has been cooked, it is still possible to use it for heating, as the wooden quarters burn slowly.

Teepee fire

Like its name, the tepee fire is made with a small pyramid of wood in the shape of a teepee or wigwam, the typical hut in the American Indians. It is a fire that burns rapidly and if the pile of wood is high enough it will soon give flames and sparks crackling in the cold night air. If using as a campfire for a small group, make sure the logs are only a foot or two in length, as it burns so quickly you will need a lot of wood. If, on the other hand, you use it for cooking, the woods must not exceed the length of fifteen centimeters. It takes a short time for the flame to rise therefore, if you make a very small teepee, this is a great way to light larger fires.

Wheel or star fire

Wheel fire, also called lazy man fire, is best lit by starting with a small pyramid fire. Due to the location of the logs, this is the type of fire that burns the slowest, consumes the least amount of wood and is easy to control. The long logs are placed like the spokes of a wheel, and only burn the ends that touch in the center. As they are consumed, the logs must be brought closer to continue to feed the fire. The more logs there are, the higher the flame will be, but three or four logs eight or ten centimeters in diameter are enough to light a cheerful fire for a small group of campers. For maximum ventilation, keep the woods from overlapping.

Hunter's fire

This is one of the most effective fires for cooking. Several stones, or two still green stumps, are arranged at a small distance from each other, so that at the narrowest end they can support the smaller pots and utensils of your field kitchen, while at the wider one, open towards the wind are about 30 cm apart.

If you use stones, be careful not to collect them from a riverbed or damp area, because the intense heat would cause the moisture contained in them to expand and the stones could crack, sending dangerous splinters and so could the pots with your dinner.

To build a hunter's fire, set up a small teepee in the center of a circle of stones or logs. If you want more draught, keep the two logs slightly raised on the side where the breeze blows, placing two wet logs underneath them, so that the air can pass underneath them as well. The efficiency of this type of fire is given by the fact that the heat is not dispersed and is reflected upwards, towards your pots and pans.

Screen fire

Screen fire is obtained by adding a structure capable of reflecting heat to a small pyramid or wheel fire. The structure can be built with different techniques and materials. By forming a small semicircle with stones or bricks, or by superimposing logs resting on two inclined poles planted in the ground.

This type of fire gives a constant heat, excellent for cooking food that will be placed on the side logs, such as a slow-cooking vertical barbecue. When placed in front of a shelter or tent, it will reflect heat to keep you warm in the evening or in bad weather.

Trench fire

This type of fire requires firm ground.

This is a hunter's fire buried in the ground, great on windy days. Dig a trench 20 cm wide, which slopes down into the ground, according to the direction of the wind, to a depth of 20, 30 cm towards the upwind end. If you must cook many courses, dig deeper and line the trench with dry stones, to better reflect the heat upwards. The pots can be placed on two sturdy green woods that will be replaced when they start to dry out and catch fire.

Pit fire or Polynesian

If you need a fire that resists the wind well and lasts several hours, this is the ideal fire. Typical of Polynesia, it is prepared by digging a well about 30 cm wide and deep. Prepare a small pyramid fire inside it with dry wood that will serve as a primer, then line the well with sloping logs about 60 cm long, so that the part in the ditch is in contact with the pyramid fire. As the ends burn, the logs will gradually and steadily descend, keeping the fire going. You will be able to plant two stakes to suspend your pot and the game is done. This fire doesn't require much maintenance, so your dinner will cook without a hitch.

Key fire

The key fire is a great way to heat and cook at the same time. A certain number of dry stones are placed on the ground so as to form a larger and a smaller circle, like a keyhole: the larger circle must be in a slight depression dug into the ground. In the center a small pyramid fire is lit, which is continued with short logs around it, forming a star. In the smallest circle a pyramid fire is prepared, and once lit it is fed with hard wood, which produces good embers to be able to cook the food. In this way we will have a fire that is always lit to heat, illuminate and possibly feed the smaller fire with other embers.

Fire-starting tools

Lighting a fire in a wild setting is not a difficult task if you have the right equipment. Therefore, having the best equipment to achieve your goal will allow you to save important energies.

Matches

Let's start with the best known and most used method in the world to light a fire: matches. The match can get wet, break, moisten and if you then use those normally called Swedish, you could ruin the brown paper to light them.
If the match is moderately damp, just pass it through your hair to dry it, but instead of having to run for cover, the best thing is to cover the head with melted wax so as to protect it. Better still would be to keep them in a watertight container such as a 35mm roll holder.

Lighter

Lighters are essentially of two types, flint and piezoelectric. The former is generally not recommended because it cannot be used with wet hands even if it has no electronic circuits, the latter until it fails just press and it turns on. Transparent models are recommended so you can see the charge level and finally the piezo-anti-wind type that doesn't make a real flame but that as long as you hold it down, they don't go out.

Firesteel

A tool that does not miss a beat and which, in principle, is satisfied with any bait, which you can hang around your neck, which you can dip, slam as much as you want, and which always works is the

Firesteel. It always works and runs out after a long time, it's easy to use, just rub the knife or any other steel tool against the bar to create the sparks needed to light a fire if we have the right tinder.

It is a rod of cerium iron which, when rubbed hard by an angular metal, generates a cascade of sparks of approximately 3632-5432 degrees °F. Coupled with a good quantity and quality of flammable material results in a safe fire. A very useful tip is to use cotton soaked in Vaseline oil, also because in addition to being very compressible it is also waterproof.

If the flammable material is missing, just scratch the bar a little and pull off a little cerium iron powder on which to let the sparks end up.

A tip, for those who use a knife, not to rub it with the blade as the high temperature that the sparks reach could compromise the edge of the blade, it is also advisable to use the back which, if not blunt, gives excellent results.

How to light the flame with the lighter:

Most flintlocks are sold with a special protective varnish on the surface, which prevents them from sparking if they inadvertently come into contact with flammable materials. To use the flint, it is necessary to remove this patina, starting to rub with not too intense pressure.

To light the fire, you will need some tinder with which to ignite the spark: wadding, charred cloth, paper, or dry wood are perfect for this function, which is obtained by scraping off the outer part of the branches and obtaining from it a sort of dry, highly flammable powder. Cotton wool and hemp twine are also very suitable. Whatever material you decide to use, it is good to pay attention to the humidity of the same, capable of totally compromising our operation. The smaller the tinder and the porous structure, the more it will be able to catch fire even at low temperatures.

If materials such as paper or cotton wool are not available, one can proceed equally with what is found in nature, such as dry leaves, grass, bark, mushrooms. After having designated our bait and prepared the flint, let's take it with one hand while holding a knife (or a rough surface) with the other and start rubbing, moving only one of the two hands and keeping the other firmly.

If you decide to use a knife to create sparks, our advice is to use the blunt side, so as not to compromise the blade and risk chipping it or even worse, cutting yourself.

It is a meticulous operation, to be carried out with diligence as the sparks could cause considerable damage if they were to fall on something other than our bait. The latter must in fact be positioned very close to the hands that are working with the lock.

To light a fire safely, you need to prepare everything you need before drawing the flint. This is because once the first sparks start to ignite, we will promptly have to approach the tinder and then immediately the wood designated for the fire.

Not all places are ideal for hosting a fire, so it is advisable to carefully choose the area to dedicate to it. It is advisable to opt for areas sheltered from the wind and mostly free, such as clearings, where the branches of the surrounding trees do not risk starting a fire.

Also keeping the right distances from shrubs, bushes and piles of dry leaves and branches can prove to be a lifesaver.

To prevent the fire from spreading, it is advisable to prepare its bed adequately, perhaps by digging slightly into the ground so that a concave point is formed where to lay the flammable material.

Following the same principle, it is possible to light a fire on a mound, created by accumulating earth under the bed of the fire so that the flames cannot reach everything around. If the area were to be particularly airy, it would be possible to repair the fire with non-flammable materials, such as damp wood.

For the spark to set fire to the tinder, we must blow gently, taking care not to extinguish it but on the contrary to feed it. In doing so we will give life to an ember of paper, wadding or other material, to be preferably positioned in the center of the bonfire so that it can gradually ignite all the rest of the wood prepared.

Our advice is to practice lighting a fire with the tinderbox over and over again, in different circumstances and climatic conditions, so that you know how to do it without a hitch in the moment of real need.

Piston Fire Starter

Another mechanically ignited tool is the Piston Fire Starter. These exploit the principle that by compressing the air, it increases in temperature. We will then be in the presence of a sealed and openable cylindrical piston. A small piece of charcloth is inserted inside, then it is closed, and the pumping begins. The heat will ignite the tinder that will be used.

Friction-based fire-starting methods

In bushcraft, there are a variety of friction ignition methods that can be used to start a fire. These methods use the friction between two materials to produce heat and create a small ember that can be blown to set the flammable material on fire.

Lighting the fire with the bow

The principle of the bow is based on friction, i.e., rubbing between two parts, between which there is friction. The bow is a very ancient lighting method and requires patience, time and effort.

We sell how to do to light a fire:

Take a green branch (flexible but resistant) at least 50 cm long and tie a rope, a lace or a loose strap to the two ends, so as to create an arch.

Wrap the string around a stick of about 30 cm with a diameter of 2 cm (non-resinous) as dry and hard as possible. The stick will act as a drill, so create a point at one end.

In order not to injure your hand and to put pressure on the stick, cover the upper point with a hard wood or a convex stone or a shell or shell.

Now, prepare a dry wooden block at least 1 cm thick, which will serve as a base.

Never use resinous wood such as pine but opt for wood such as willow or poplar.

On the wider side of the tablet, dig a shallow hole in the upper part (at least 1 cm from the edge), while in the lower part corresponding to the hole, make an inverted V-shaped groove, which will serve to collect the dust produced by rubbing the tablet. bow with board.

It is precisely in this blackish powder produced that the spark would form.

Insert the stick into the hole in the table and, keeping it still with your foot, rotate the drill by moving the bow back and forth (as if it were sawing).

When you smell burning, increase the speed.

The drill runs better when lubricated with a little grease. If it is too stiff, you need to twist some more rope around it.

While carrying out the movement, do not stop otherwise the area would cool down immediately and you would have to start over.

When enough blackish dust has accumulated in the V-shaped groove, blow slowly into the groove and bring the tinder closer. When the flame is created add more tinder and then the firewood.

Hand-to-hand ignition technique

The hand-to-hand fire-starting method is a fire-starting technique that involves using your hands to roll a piece of dry wood against a log to produce heat and ignite a flammable material.

The technique consists in rotating the drill in your hands, so that one of the two ends rotates inside a circular cavity made on another piece of wood which is called the base. The friction simultaneously produces heat and wood dust which turns into embers as the temperature increases.

The first step, therefore, consists in identifying a piece of dry and resistant wood, approximately 30-45 cm long and 2-3 cm in diameter. This piece of wood will be used as a drill.

The choice of suitable essences is fundamental in this type of technique; some types of wood allow easier and faster ignition and it is good to try to save energy if you have the possibility. In general, soft woods should be preferred for the base and slightly harder woods for the drill. Soft means that they should be able to be incised by pressing against them with the thumbnail.

Before starting, immediately prepare a nest of dry grass in which you will deposit your embers. Additional flammable material can be inserted inside the nest which will facilitate combustion.

Subsequently, a soft and slightly inclined block of wood is chosen, which serves as the basis to produce heat. For example, you can use a tree trunk cut in half, or a large palm leaf.

At this point, the piece of dry wood is placed on top of the softwood block and the piece of wood is started to roll between the hands, exerting constant pressure and pushing the piece of wood back and forth on the softwood block. This friction produces heat, which heats the flammable material under the piece of wood.

By continuing to roll the piece of wood with your hands, enough heat is generated to ignite a small ember, which can be blown to ignite the flammable material. Once the embers have formed, other flammable materials, such as dry leaves, thin twigs or birch bark, can be added to make the fire grow.

Fire piston ignition method

The "fire piston" ignition method is a fire ignition technique that uses the principle of air compression to generate heat and ignite a flammable material.

The fire piston consists of a hollow metal or wooden tube, inside which there is a piston. The end of the tube is closed with a rubber or cork stopper, which forms an airtight seal when the piston is pushed into the tube.

To start a fire with the fire piston, a piece of flammable material, such as charred cotton or amadou, is inserted into the end of the tube, near the cap seal. Subsequently, the piston is pushed inside the tube with a strong pressure, generating a rapid compression of the air inside the tube. This compression produces such high heat that the flammable material at the end of the tube ignites.

Once the flammable material is ignited, the embers are gently fanned to grow the fire and add more flammable material.

The fire piston method of lighting takes some practice to master, but once mastered, it can be a quick and efficient method of starting a fire in any weather condition, even in windy or rainy weather.

Other primitive fire-starting methods

There are many primitive methods of making fire that have been used since ancient times before the invention of modern lighters and matches. Some of the more common include:

Magnifying glass and sun rays

To start a fire with the loupe, you need some tools and a sunny day.

Here are the steps to do it:

- Find a magnifying glass. It is important that it is a convex lens and not flat, so that it can concentrate the sunlight in a single point.
- Collect flammable material. You can use dry twigs, dry leaves, paper, cotton, straw, dry grass, etc.
- Prepare flammable material. Chop the material into small pieces or make it flat and thin so that it burns easily.
- Find a sunny spot and position the lens so that the sunlight is concentrated in one spot. Focuses sunlight on flammable material. It will take some time to get enough heat to burn the material.
- When the material begins to burn, blow it gently to increase the flames. Gradually add larger material to create a bigger fire.

Flint

Flint is a rock that is used to generate sparks used to make fire. It is composed primarily of iron minerals, such as magnetite, which can generate sparks when rubbed against another hard material such as steel. The flint has been used since ancient times for lighting fire, when man learned to use it to produce sparks and make the fire flare up.

The flint most used initially was pyrite proper, i.e., monomeric iron bisulphide. It was usually of a color and luster like that of gold, hard and not subject to decomposition into flakes like other minerals with similar characteristics.

It was subsequently replaced by flint which, despite having the defects of having to be suitably shaped and breaking more easily, produced sparks in less time.

To use a flint to start a fire, follow these steps:
- Gather flammable material, such as dry leaves, thin twigs, birch bark, or similar material.
- Find flint, which is a hard, dark rock with a rough surface.
- Prepare the flint by rubbing it with a piece of steel or iron. Use the sharp or serrated side of the piece of metal to strike sparks on the surface of the flint. Alternatively, you can use a specially designed fire starter to start a fire.
- Place the flammable material on a flat, stable surface.
- Use flint and steel to create sparks and direct these sparks at the flammable material. If you are successful, sparks will land on the material and set it ablaze.
- Stack flammable material with twigs and other progressively larger fuels to fuel the fire and make it grow.

It is important to be patient and persistent in the process of starting a fire with a flint, as it can take some time and practice to get sparks large enough to ignite flammable material.

Making fire with the belt method

It is possible to light the fire with a belt. You need to place a branch resting it on a boulder so that it is slightly raised at one end. Under it we will have to place the combustible material. With the belt, however, we have to wrap the piece of wood so that it remains in the center and that the ends of the belt are in our hands. At this point with continuous and fast movements we have to rub the belt on the wood until enough heat is created to set the underlying material. It is similar to if you want to make a percussive fire.

Safety rules for lighting a fire

The first thing to consider when thinking about lighting a fire is safety rules. Everyone wants to be able to create a nice bonfire to keep warm by, but no one wants to be trapped in a wildfire.

The size of your fire doesn't have to be large: a small fire is much easier to manage, will require less materials to maintain and will give you even better results.

Make sure that the place chosen to light the bonfire is well prepared: you must remove any combustible (dry branches, leaves, weeds) within a three-meter radius.

Always try to foresee that the flame could spread, avoid lighting a fire in places surrounded by shrubs, branches and plants.

Always keep a container of water or other material capable of extinguishing the flame near you.

The place you choose for your flame is crucial. A good practice requires that the fire be lit inside a pit at least 10 centimeters deep and surrounded by stones. Once the bonfire is extinguished because you leave the place, be sure to cover the ashes with the excavated earth and put all the stones you moved back in their place, so as not to spoil the place for those who arrive after you.

Where to find fuel to make fire

The first step to starting a fire is to acquire the right material. If you are in a forest or in a natural area, especially when the climate is dry, it will be very easy: just collect dry branches and twigs of assorted sizes, the thinner ones will be useful for lighting and the more robust ones for maintenance.

If there are rivers nearby, chances are you will find plenty of material along its banks, as the current causes the wood to pile up and then lie ashore to dry out during times of low flow.

The lowest part of the shrubs often has dry branches that are easy to harvest.

Rotten wood is perfect for burning; in rainy areas you can find it in the hollows of logs.

If you are in wet areas, you may need to dry the branches before using them. If the rain is not so much, just remove the outer part of the bark and the wood inside will be dry and ready to burn. If, on the other hand, the rain is abundant and you only find wet wood, you will have to cut the branches lengthwise and use the fragments thus obtained. If there is already a fire burning, you can dry the new wood thanks to it.

Chapter 2: Water Procurement and Purification

Water is the resource that keeps us alive and must absolutely be found and made drinkable within a maximum period of 24 hours. Without food, it is possible to survive for a few days, but without water, dehydration occurs, and death occurs in a rather short time. In some places finding water will not be a problem since streams and waterways abound in some natural oases, but obviously it will not be possible to drink it before having subjected it to a purification process.

The water in question, in fact, could be rich in dangerous bacteria which, if ingested, could trigger serious health problems, such as infections, diseases, salmonella and many other annoying and dangerous ailments. To make the water drinkable, it is possible to create natural filters capable of retaining the largest impurities, which will be used for several days to be more effective.

The importance of water in survival situations

Water is even more necessary for survival than food and an adult man must drink about two liters of water a day, an amount that increases in the event of physical fatigue or climatic conditions such as high atmospheric temperatures.

Water plays many roles within our body, all of vital importance such as correct hydration of the body, elimination of toxins and toxic waste for our body, body thermoregulation and correct transport of nutrients also useful for proper digestion.

Also know that the need for water does not decrease as temperatures drop. It is true that you sweat less, but in any case, you still lose enough fluids through skin perspiration due to dry air. You also need to drink more when there is strong wind.

What happens to our body if we don't take the right amount of water? When the amount of water in the body is not sufficient, dehydration occurs. When there is severe dehydration, the cells of our body tend to shrink and consequently the normal flow of blood, and therefore of oxygen, within our muscles is interrupted. Dehydration begins after 6 continuous hours of lack of water and, after 24 hours, know that you are in a situation of grave danger to your life.

Water is also important for many other bushcraft activities, such as cooking, cleaning tools, and personal hygiene. It is important to carry enough water with you to meet your needs and, if possible, find sources of water along the way.

In general, water is one of the most critical elements to survival in any bushcraft situation, and it is important to have the knowledge and skills to find and purify it safely and effectively.

Once you understand the vital importance of water, it will therefore be clear to you that the place to choose to build your shelter must be as close to a source of water.

Sources of water in the wilderness

There are several sources of water that can be easily found in nature. Let's see what the main sources are, that is, the ones you will find more easily.

- Rivers. Rivers are bodies of water that flow through the earth and join together to form the great rivers that feed lakes and oceans.
- Lakes. Lakes are large bodies of water that form naturally in the earth, often through the creation of natural dams or the deposition of sediments.
- Springs. Springs are points where groundwater rises to the surface. They can be small pools or large rivers.
- Aquifers. Aquifers are layers of permeable soil or rock that contain groundwater.
- Wells. Wells are holes dug in the earth to draw underground water.
- Rain. Rain is a natural source of water that recharges rivers, lakes and aquifers.
- Snow and ice. Snow and ice can melt and supply water to underlying streams.
- In fruit. Fruit and plant species contain large amounts of water. Some species are edible by humans and one of the simplest ways to quench your thirst is to collect fruit. Coconuts, for example, contain water rich in vitamins and mineral salts, and the pulp is an excellent food, but oranges, pineapples, mangoes, lemons and so on also help to satisfy water needs.
- Bamboo sticks. Even green bamboo can drip water when bent.

Flowing water sources are the best option, as the movement doesn't allow bacteria to rot. This means that small streams of water should be looked for first. Rivers are acceptable but remember that larger ones are often more polluted than smaller ones. Before you collect water from the river though, make sure there are no dead animal carcasses or droppings.

To find rivers, lakes and streams you need to follow the points where the vegetation is greener or, for example, follow the animals (birds, mammals, bees, ants, a path recently beaten by animals or the presence of excrement near a crack). If you are surrounded by a mountain range, the water usually collects in the less inclined base because the flow is slower. The caves are created of water, inspecting them to the bottom you can find streams of water. Narrow gorges and crevasses can give birth to small springs. Avoid digging in porous and friable soils as the water accumulates too deeply in those cases.

By digging in certain places, such as dry riverbeds, dry lakes, valleys, wetlands, green areas, it might be possible to accumulate water inside holes or to concentrate small streams of water; in these cases, it is still necessary to boil or purify the water. There are some plants that love water such as willows, elders, reeds, water lilies. An excavation can be attempted in their vicinity to find water.

In the greener and brighter grassy areas where the stems are tall and fleshy, an excavation can be attempted as the soil is certainly moist and there is the possibility of finding water. Fresh water can often be found behind the sand dunes along the sea.

Water purification methods

The first thing to know is that there are many ways to get drinking water. It is important to pay attention to all types of water that can be found in nature and to avoid drinking it unless you are sure that it is not from contaminated sources.

Therefore, never drink from pools of stagnant water, where the vegetation is strange or absent and, obviously, do not drink sea water: the salt present in the water dehydrates the body and can be very harmful. It is also advisable not to eat snow and ice, because they cause heat loss in the body: it is better to collect some and melt them in a saucepan until boiling, so that the water obtained is also purified.

When purification tablets or special kits are not available, techniques can be used to obtain water to drink safely. Some systems are simpler, others more difficult to implement and require some experience to implement. Let's see together the simplest methods to obtain drinking water in situations of need, remembering that it is never advisable to drink from unknown sources. Yes, instead to the collection by condensation of water vapor or to the use of rain.

Here are the best ways to purify water in nature:

Purify water with the classic method: boiling

Boiling is one of the oldest methods. And perhaps the safest of all. Boiling water can eliminate most of the pathogenic bacteria, viruses and parasites that may be present.

Start by collecting water. Get water from a reliable source, such as a river, lake, or stream. Avoid collecting water from ponds or waterholes, which may contain more impurities. If possible, filter the water through a cloth or filter to remove sediment and larger particles.

Place the water in a heatproof container and bring it to a boil over medium-high heat. Let the water boil for 1 to 3 minutes. Boiling time varies according to altitude.

If you don't have a metal container, you can build one from the bark of a birch tree in which you will insert rocks made incandescent by fire.

After boiling, let the water cool completely before drinking. Once the water has boiled, it should be safe to drink. However, it should be noted that boiling water does not remove all chemicals, heavy metals and other contaminants.

Boil water with hot rocks

If you don't have a saucepan available, it is still possible to boil water with a very simple trick. You need to take two large enough pieces of wood and dig two cavities of the desired size inside. Both must be filled with the collected water. At this point a fire is lit with twigs of wood, taking care to feed it so that the flame is constant. Then some stones are taken and put on the fire, so that they become red-hot. Once they become incandescent, they must be taken one by one using a branch as if it were pliers and placed in the first container for a few seconds, so that the impurities are eliminated. When the stone is clean but still hot, it will be placed in the second container: the accumulation of stones will boil the water and make it drinkable.

The distillation of water

Water distillation is a water purification process that involves heating water until it evaporates, then condensing the vapor into clean liquid water. The distillation process exploits the fact that most of the impurities present in the water do not evaporate together with the water, but remain in the original container, while the pure water vapor rises to the top.

The distillation process can remove many of the unwanted substances found in water, including minerals, heavy metals, bacteria, viruses, chlorine and other chemicals. Distillation is an effective method of obtaining pure water from contaminated water, but it takes time and energy to evaporate the water and cool the water vapor.

There are different types of water distillation, but all involve a heat source to evaporate the water, followed by a cooling system to condense the vapor into liquid water.

The system used to distill water in nature will allow you to obtain purified water from 500 ml up to 2 liters in 24 hours.

After you find a suitable place to collect water, such as a stream, river, or pool of water, you need to dig a shallow hole, about 3 feet deep and 3 feet wide, in the ground near the water. The hole should be large enough to hold a container for water and deep enough to allow a smaller container to be placed in it.

Place a clean, heat-resistant container inside the hole. The container should be large enough to hold the water you wish to distill. Then cover the hole with a sheet of heat-resistant plastic. The plastic should be positioned so that it rests against the edges of the hole, creating a slight depression in the center.

Then place a weight in the center of the plastic sheet, so that the sheet descends towards the water collection container.

Make sure the hole is placed in the sun, so that the solar heat warms and evaporates the water. The water will evaporate, condense on the plastic and flow towards the center, where it will fall into the smaller container.

Collect the collected distilled water in the smaller container, which should be placed in the center of the hole. The distilled water obtained this way will not be completely free of impurities, but it should be safe to drink.

Remember that distilling water in nature takes time and patience, and the resulting water may not be completely free of impurities. If you could obtain safe drinking water from reliable sources, it's always better to do so than relying on distillation.

How to build a water filter

Building a water filter is one of the basic bushcraft skills and can be done with natural materials that can be found in nature.

Here are the steps to follow to build a water filter:

- Find an empty container such as a plastic bottle, jar, or heavy-duty bag.
- Fill the container with a layer of charcoal or ash. This layer helps remove contaminants from the water.
- Add a layer of sand over the charcoal. This layer helps filter out larger particles from the water.
- Add a layer of gravel on top of the sand. This layer helps filter out even larger particles from the water.
- Place the filter over a clean container to collect the filtered water.
- Pour the water to be filtered on the filter.
- Repeat the process until you have enough filtered water for your needs.

How to collect and store water

Collect rainwater

A simple and immediate method is to collect rainwater through containers. If you don't have containers available, you can build a canopy with a small channel with branches and leaves, which conveys rainwater into a single container.

Another ingenious system consists in rolling a cloth or a t-shirt around the trunk of a tree, leaving one end hanging towards the ground. The fabric will collect the water that drips into the container underneath. Finally, if you have a waterproof tarp, just dig a hole in the ground and cover it with the tarp, on the bottom of which the rain will collect. Once collected, it will still be necessary to boil it in a container for ten minutes to make it drinkable.

How to collect water in a swamp

Collecting water from a swamp can be a difficult and potentially dangerous task, as swamps can contain stagnant and contaminated water, which could cause disease. However, if you have the appropriate tools and follow a few precautions, you can safely collect water from the bog.

Use a clean container: Use a clean container, such as a bucket or pitcher, to catch the water. This way you avoid contaminating the water with dirt or debris.

Sterilize the container: Before using the container to collect water, you can sterilize it with a disinfectant solution, such as javel water. This will reduce the risk of contamination.

Choosing the Right Area: Choose an area of the swamp where the water looks cleaner and clearer.

Filter the water: Once the water has collected, you can filter it with a clean tissue or cheesecloth to remove any particles or debris.

Purify water: To eliminate bacteria and parasites from collected water, you can use a purification system, such as chlorine tablets or a water filter.

Boil the water: Boiling the water for at least 10 minutes will kill any bacteria or parasites and make the water safe to drink.

Practice personal safety: When collecting water from a bog, wear protective clothing such as long pants, waterproof boots, and gloves. Avoid entering deep water or approaching wildlife that may be present in the swamp.

Collect plant transpiration

Another easy option for harvesting water is to take advantage of plant transpiration.

This is the process in which moisture is transported from the roots of a plant to the underside of its leaves. From there, it vaporizes into the atmosphere. And it is before the vaporization process that you are going to collect the water.

First thing in the morning, tie a plastic bag around a green, leafy branch or shrub.

During the day, the plant perspires and produces moisture. However, instead of vaporizing in the atmosphere, the water will collect at the bottom of the bag. But be careful never to do this process with a poisonous plant.

Collect water from snow and ice

Especially in the mountains, snow and ice are abundant in the winter months, and sometimes even available all year round.

Snow and ice provide an excellent source of water; however, they should always be melted before drinking.

Eating snow and ice directly will lower your body temperature, which will quickly lead you to dehydration as it forces your metabolism to speed up to keep you warm.

Here's how to get drinking water from snow:

- Gather snow from a clean, pristine area away from sources of pollution. Avoid collecting snow that has a yellow or brown tint, as it may contain contaminants.
- Melt the collected snow by bringing it to a boil in a heatproof container. Boil the snow for at least 5 minutes to eliminate any contaminants and bacteria.
- After melting the snow, or ice, strain the water through a cloth or filter to remove any sediment or particles. If you don't have a filter, you can use a clean cloth or mesh to filter the water.
- After filtration, let the water cool before drinking.

- Before drinking the water, make sure the water is drinkable. If you don't have a water test kit available, use one to check the water quality. If not, you can rely on your senses: if the water tastes or smells funny, don't drink it.

In general, snow can be an excellent source of drinking water in an emergency, but it's important to follow these steps to ensure your water is safe to drink.

Chapter 3: Food Procurement

The importance of food in survival situations

Food is a fundamental factor for survival in any situation, and this also applies in the case of emergencies or survival in the wild.

Food provides our body with the energy needed to carry out daily activities, maintain body temperature and, in general, survive. In emergency or survival situations in the wild, food becomes even more important because our body's energy reserves can be rapidly depleted, especially if we are forced to perform intense physical activities such as walking, building a shelter or looking for water.

Furthermore, the intake of adequate food and water can have a significant impact on our state of mental and physical health. Hunger and dehydration can in fact cause fatigue, tiredness, irritability, concentration problems and even hallucinations.

It is therefore important to know the food sources available in nature, such as edible wild plants, fishing, hunting or collecting insects, in order to be able to supplement the food that is brought with you or replace it if necessary. Furthermore, it is important to have a food plan and choose foods that provide adequate energy intake and essential nutrients for our body.

Finally, it is important to underline that in emergency or survival situations in the wild, food safety must always be a priority. It is important to avoid eating suspicious foods or foods of unknown origin, to prevent poisoning and food poisoning which could further jeopardize the emergency situation.

Edible plants and fruits

Recognizing edible plants in the wild can be a very useful skill in emergency or survival situations, but it requires a good understanding of plants and identification techniques.

Here are some useful tips to recognize edible plants in nature:

- Refer to plant recognition guides. There are many guides available on the market describing edible wild plants, their distinctive characteristics and nutritional properties. Look for a guide specific to your geographic area to be sure the plants you are looking for are present in your area.
- Pay attention to the flowers, leaves and fruit of the plant. Look closely at the shape, color, and arrangement of the plant's flowers, leaves, and fruit. These can be important clues in identifying the plant.
- Smell and taste. The smell and taste of plants can be helpful in identifying them.
- Avoid toxic plants. There are many toxic plants in nature that can cause poisoning or intoxication. Learn about the most common toxic plants by reading guides before venturing out and be sure to avoid picking them.
- Be aware of your environment. The type of edible plants presents in an area can depend on the climate, soil and type of habitat. Try to understand your environment and the plants that inhabit it to have a better chance of finding edible plants.
- Do not pick protected or endangered plants. Before harvesting wild plants, make sure they are not protected by environmental laws or endangered.

Before eating any plant, it is important to be sure of its identity and nutritional properties. If in doubt, avoid picking or eating it.

Now let's see which plants are the edible fruits that you can find in nature.

- Dandelion. Any part of the dandelion can be eaten at any time of the year, but preferably before the flower buds appear.
- Reed Dog or Typha latifolia. It is easily recognized by its large flowers and inflorescences. The whole plant can be eaten, but it is best eaten in late fall before the stems wither. It's best to start with the roots and stems close to the ground.
- The burdock. Burdock is often seen as an unsightly weed, but in many parts of the world it is grown for its roots. The roots are dug up until they are finely chopped for cooking. For cooking, the skin is not removed from the roots. Only the roots of young plants in the first year of life can be eaten raw; otherwise, they must be cooked in the same way as carrots and potatoes.
- Arrowroot (Maranta root). The root is usually dried and ground into a powder, but it can also be cooked and eaten like any other vegetable.
- Prickly pear. Part of one of the large edible plants, it is most found in arid areas, but don't be surprised if you find it in other places as well. Opuntia leaves and fruits are grown as food in many parts of the world and in many countries. Fruits are also a good source of water. The spines of fruits and leaves should be shaved before eating. The leaves can be grated, peeled and cooked in hot oil or salted.

- The hawthorn berries. they are edible but harmful to the digestive system. This fruit can be eaten by scraping the skin with the teeth. However, make sure you don't eat hawthorn berries if you experience any unusual symptoms such as dizziness, migraines or skin rashes. Not only do they have heart-healthy properties, such as lowering high blood pressure and atherosclerosis, but they also have antioxidant properties that help boost the immune system.
- Miner's lettuce. It grows wild almost everywhere. It can be eaten as a green salad. Miner's lettuce is found almost everywhere, including in the shade and on riverbanks. Miner's lettuce owes its name to the California Gold Rush. Gold miners ate it to ward off scurvy.
- The Pinon Nuts. Pinon Nuts grow wild in eastern North America, but if you harvest them (in the shell), you'll have to remove them because the shells get harder to remove as they dry out. Black walnuts are very flavorful, so if you live in an area with a high concentration of black walnut trees. Many of the black walnuts come from wild trees, unlike English walnuts they come mainly from orchards. They contain the highest amount of protein of all nuts.
- The tops of Milkweed. The young shoots of thistle can be eaten, but it is better to cook them in boiling water. The buds, stems and shoots are edible. It is a myth that they must be cooked repeatedly in fresh water to remove toxins and bitterness. This is certainly possible, but it's a waste of water and time. The young stems, shoots and seeds can be eaten raw. They are only available during late summer and early fall before the pinecones open and produce seeds.
- Pine nuts. All kinds of pine nuts can be eaten. You can also consume other parts of the pine, such as the bark and needles, which can be steeped in hot water to make a vitamin-rich tea. If you place an unopened pinecone near a heat source, it will open, and berry cones will fall out. They can be eaten raw or roasted. All types of nuts are good meat substitutes because they are high in protein and fat. They are also good for heart health and contain vitamin E.
- Wild strawberries. Recognizing them is easy since they are very similar to their cultivated relatives, but in a miniaturized version.
- Blueberries. They are the fruit of medium and high mountains (they grow up to almost 2000 meters) and ripen in July and August.
- Wild blackberries. Wild blackberries are a variety of berries that grow wild in many parts of the world. Wild blackberries are easily recognized by their ball or cone shape, bumpy surface, and black or dark purple coloration. They grow on brambles, generally along the edges of the woods, in the prairies and along the roads. To collect wild blackberries, it is important to use gloves to protect your hands from the thorns of the brambles. It's also important to choose only ripe, healthy blackberries and leave any that are still unripe or diseased.
- Wild raspberries. Wild raspberries are a variety of berries that grow wild in many parts of the world, especially in temperate climate areas. Wild raspberries are easily recognized by their shape resembling a small lamp, with a point at the end. They grow on bushes and shrubs, particularly

along forest edges, in grasslands and along roadsides. Wild raspberries are usually ripe and ready to pick in late summer or early fall.
- Silene swollen. The swollen silene, also known as threaded silene or Silene's egg, is an annual or biennial herbaceous plant that grows in Europe, Asia and North Africa. It is known for its distinctive bubble-shaped, swollen fruit that resembles an egg and contains brown or black seeds. The swollen silene grows in dry soils, on meadows and in rocky areas. The most interesting part of the plant is its swollen fruit, which can be harvested and cooked as a vegetable or as an ingredient in soups or stews. The flavor of the fruit is sweet and delicate and recalls that of peas or broad beans.

Hunting and trapping game

Hunting is one of the traditional bushcraft skills, and can be useful in survival situations where you are trying to get your own food. However, it is important to note that hunting must be conducted with respect for the animals and in compliance with local hunting laws.

Hunting is an activity that man has practiced since prehistoric times, it was for long periods one of the major sources of food supply for the sustenance of the human population.

One of the first rules of survival is: avoid useless efforts, in this case we must try not to consume more energy in hunting than we would recover by eating our prey.

Hunting is an art; we must use all our senses and skills to surprise our prey and be able to capture it. Observing tracks, recognizing noises, understanding the habits of the prey. We have to catch her off guard and catch her when she least expects it.

There are many hunting methods used in bushcraft, but some of the more common ones include:

Bow and Arrow Hunting

As we have seen, bow and arrow hunting requires some skill and practice, but can be very effective for hunting medium to small game.

Hunting with a bow and arrow takes great skill and practice but can be a very effective hunting technique. Here are the general steps for hunting with a bow and arrow:

- Before you begin, practice aiming it's important to be accurate in aiming when hunting with a bow and arrow. Regularly practice aiming at stationary targets, such as balloons or archery targets.
- Choice of Bow and Arrows: Choose a bow and arrows that suit your needs and strength.
- Identify the Animal: Try to locate the animals in their hunting area. Learn to recognize animal cues, such as footprints, droppings, and food tracks.
- Get close to the animal: Try to get as close to the animal as possible without being noticed. Move slowly and carefully, trying to stay out of the way of trees and rocks.
- Shot: When you are close enough to the animal, prepare for the shot. Try to hit the animal in the vital area, such as the heart or lungs. Try to make an accurate and deadly blow to reduce the animal's suffering.
- Retrieve the prey: if you hit the animal, try to recover it as fast as possible. Follow the trail of blood, if any, to find your prey. If you can't find the prey or if you have injured the animal but not killed it, try to treat it with respect and humanity.

Hunting with snares or snaring

this method involves using a snare to capture the animal. The trap consists of a snare which is fixed to the ground and then pulled by hand when the animal passes.

To hunt with snares, you need to locate an area where the animal moves regularly, such as a pass, trail, or area where the animal searches for food. Once the area has been identified, traps can be set to capture the animal.

There are several snaring techniques, but in general, the idea is to build a trap that allows the animal to stick its head or leg into a snare and then become trapped. Snares can be made of a variety of materials, such as wire or rope, but it's important that they're strong enough to hold the animal once it's caught. To catch the animal, it is important that the trap is placed correctly and that the animal does not detect it. Furthermore, it is important to check the traps regularly to prevent the animal from being trapped for too long.

Crossbow Hunting

The crossbow is a weapon like the bow, but with a shorter string and greater firepower. Hunting with a crossbow requires more skill than a bow and arrow but can be very effective for hunting medium to large game.

When you are hunting animals remember that:

- When following an animal, walk with the sun behind you, as animals tend not to turn towards it so as not to blind themselves.
- Mask your perfume: wash off the sweat well or let yourself be enveloped by the smoke for a few minutes.
- If the animal turns to your side or stares at you, remain completely still until it resumes the activity it was carrying out.
- Walk with a soft step, placing your toe first to feel the ground and avoid dry leaves or twigs that could make noise.
- Always move against the wind.
- Always prefer early morning for hunting.
- Wounded animals can become very aggressive so be prepared to defend yourself.

Fishing and gathering seafood

Fish, especially in sea areas and in the presence of rivers and lakes, are an important source of food that should not be overlooked.

Fish is an excellent food, it contains a lot of proteins, it is rich in vitamins and mineral salts, and it is low in fat. Fish also contains Omega-3.

Fish can be caught in several ways:

- With bare hands: this simple and primitive technique can be used in a river. The technique consists in taking the fish from underneath with two hands and throwing it towards the shore, once on land you have to immobilize it before the fish wriggles and manages to return to the water. Move slowly and keep your hands in the water making very few movements, avoid casting your shadow on the fish. You can also create a barrier and lead the fish towards it, to make it easier to catch.

- With lances and harpoons: this technique is advisable in shallow waters and if there are many fish. The technique consists in holding the spear on the surface of the water and when a fish passes by, stabbing it with a lightning movement (sometimes it takes hours to succeed if you are a beginner, so don't lose heart). An excellent harpoon can be made by shaping the ends of the harpoon with teeth to prevent the fish from escaping once caught.
- With traps or with the net: with these techniques we could catch fish in quantity without too much effort. If you have a net (if you have time, you can also weave one) just place it in the water following the current of the river. We can also make traps to block the fish that end up in them (for example with cages, or with stones or large wood to divert the fish towards capture areas).
- With hook and wire: the hook can be improvised with wire, bones, nails, safety pins, needles, clips, thorns, boot buckles. For the line, snares, ropes, wire (nylon would be ideal) are fine, even made with vegetable materials. To be successful with this very rudimentary type of fishing you need to have patience and a lot of attention: we will have to let the hook dangle in the water remaining very close to the diving point, so as to immediately notice if and when a fish will bite, pulling it up before it can escape.

For the bait you can use insects (winged ants and crickets), worms, small fish, larvae, entrails and scraps of animals. The most used live baits are earthworms and caterpillars of blow wort. You have to place them on the hook so that they can move freely, without killing them. You can also use dead baits such as corn, fruit, bread, or some artisanal pasta made with particularly strong ingredients such as cheese. Here are some useful tips for easy fishing:

✓ Fish are attracted to shady areas of waterways.
✓ Night fishing can be done with the use of a flashlight (it can be very fruitful).
✓ Prefer fishing before sunrise and just after sunset.
✓ You can attract fish to your spear by attaching a fish-shaped lure carved from cedar or willow wood to it.
✓ Fishing takes a lot of patience, especially if you practice it with makeshift means, don't be discouraged if you can't get results, try and try again and with experience you will become better and better.
✓ The best ones can also fish with a bow and arrow.
✓ Never eat the internal organs of fish.
✓ If the method you use to fish has given you satisfactory results, always use that.

As for seafood, harvesting can be dangerous if you don't know the risks associated with harvesting these foods. Here are some tips for harvesting seafood:

- Choose only safe collection areas. It is important to be careful and choose safe collection areas where the water is clean and free from contaminants.
- Know about seafood: It is important to know the various species of seafood and how to identify them. This can help avoid harvesting protected or health-threatening species.
- Use Proper Gear: Some seafood species can be difficult to harvest without the use of proper gear. These can include nets, rakes and buckets. It is important to use tools that do not damage the habitat and do not compromise the survival of the species collected.
- Storage: Once seafood has been harvested, it is important to store it properly to prevent it from spoiling or becoming contaminated. This may include storing in cold water or transporting in an airtight container with ice to maintain freshness.

Preparation and cooking methods

Game preparation in bushcraft can vary depending on the species of animal, available resources and personal preferences. However, there are a few basic methods that can be used to prepare game in bushcraft. Here are some of them:

- Skinning: After killing the animal, the first thing to do is remove the skin. This can be done by using a sharp knife to cut the skin around the animal's legs and neck, then pulling the skin away from the body. A sharp stone may also be used to aid in the removal of the skin.
- Evisceration: Once the skin has been removed, the animal's innards must be removed. This can be done by opening the animal's abdominal cavity and removing its internal organs. This operation must be done carefully to avoid breaking the organs and contaminating the meat.
- Cleaning: Once the animal has been skinned and eviscerated, it is necessary to clean the meat of the excess parts and hair left on the meat. This can be done by using cold water and rubbing the meat with your hands.

As for the fish, here's how to clean it:
- Remove the scales: with a knife, gently scrape the scales off the fish, starting from the tail and working towards the head. Scales can also be removed using a knife or scale remover.
- Cut off the head: With a sharp knife, cut off the head of the fish, being careful not to cut into the flesh. This can be done by making a cut behind the gills.
- Gut the fish: using the knife, make a cut from the anus to the throat of the fish, extract the innards and throw them away. Rinse the inside of the fish well with cold water to remove any residue.

- Remove the fins: with a pair of scissors or a knife, cut off the lateral and dorsal fins. If desired, the tail fin can also be removed.
- Wash the fish: rinse the fish under running cold water to remove any traces of blood or residue.

Furthermore, it is important to avoid throwing the innards or fins into the water, in order not to pollute the surrounding environment.

Once you have your game you can:

- ✓ Boil the meat for at least an hour: however, the times vary according to the type of meat and the size of the pieces; take a look when it becomes tender enough and you see it well cooked, remove it.
- ✓ Boil: after boiling water, bring the temperature to a few degrees below 100 degrees and put the meat in.
- ✓ Roasting: put the meat cut into small pieces on a skewer and turn it over the hot embers, avoid burning the outside too much and make sure you cook the inside well.
- ✓ In the oven: make a hole and put the meat in a wrapping made of leaves or aluminum foil, cover the hole and light the fire above it.
- ✓ Steam: still in a hole put the embers at the bottom and alternate layers of food with broad leaves or moss, then seal the hole.
- ✓ Frying: place a stone slab over the fire and when it gets hot, put the meat on it, turning it several times until it's cooked through. Remember if blood comes out when you squeeze the meat, it isn't cooked yet.
- ✓ Smoking: expose the food to smoke, derived from the combustion of wood, take care that the flame does not touch the food.
- ✓ Dry in the sun: arrange the food on a surface, better if metal or, if necessary, on a sheet or cloth. Let it dry in the sun, turning it from time to time.
- ✓ Dry in the wind: in this case the food must be stored in the shade, it must not meet the sun's rays and must be placed in a ventilated area. Air drying is slower, but the product remains softer.

As for cooking fish, here are the best methods:

- ✓ Cooking on a hot stone: Find a flat, clean stone and heat it over a fire. When the stone is hot enough, place the fish or seafood directly on the stone and cook until cooked through. This cooking method is very fast and allows you to avoid the use of kitchen utensils.
- ✓ Cooking in a natural oven: build a natural oven with stones, wood and mud and place the fish or seafood inside. The fire will need to burn for some time to create enough heat, then about 20-30 minutes will be enough to cook the food.
- ✓ Cooking on a Grill: Build a portable grill out of branches and wire and cook your fish or seafood on top of it.

PART 3: TRAPPING 101

Chapter 1: Trapping

The importance of trapping in bushcraft

Bushcraft trapping is an important skill because it allows you to get food from nature. In many survival situations, catching wild food may be the only way to obtain the nourishment needed to survive.

Catching wild animals such as fish, game or shellfish can provide essential proteins for the body. The ability to catch their own food also allows them to reduce their dependence on pre-packaged food or external food sources, increasing autonomy and food security.

In addition, bushcrafting food capture also requires an understanding of the life cycle of wild animals and the seasonality of foods, which can lead to greater awareness of the natural surroundings. This can promote a more sustainable and environmentally friendly lifestyle, contributing to the conservation of natural ecosystems.

In summary, bushcraft trapping is a core skill that allows you to acquire food from nature, increase self-reliance and food security, and develop greater awareness of the natural environment.

Types of traps

When you're out in the wild without a handy tool to help you hunt for food, you still fall into primitive traps.

Traps are devices that capture animals humanely and without causing them suffering. Traps can be hand made using natural materials, such as wood and rope, or can be purchased from specialty stores. Traps are placed in areas where animals move, such as paths or food sources, and can be checked regularly to release captured animals.

There are many types of traps, but they all have in common the goal of catching animals in a humane way and without causing them suffering or permanent damage.

Here are some of the more common traps used in bushcraft:

Bow Trap

Bow traps are a type of trap used in bushcraft for catching small game animals. These traps consist of a wooden or metal bow, fixed to the ground or a tree, and a string or nylon thread stretched between the bow and a lever. The lever acts as a trap activator: when an animal touches the lever, the bow releases and the string or nylon line tightens around the animal, trapping it.

Arc traps are considered death traps, as the trapped animal can be seriously injured or killed by the trap mechanism itself. For this reason, Arc Traps must be used carefully and responsibly. If you want to create an arc trap you will need a bow, a nylon string or thread, a lever, an activator (for example, a rod or stone), and a few nails or screws to fasten the elements together. The bow can be made from a flexible branch of wood, such as ash or hazel, or a piece of metal or plastic.

If you decide to build the bow out of wood, choose a flexible branch about 60-90 cm long and thick enough to withstand the tension of the string. Remove any knots and side branches. Bend the bow into a U shape and fix it in this position with nails or screws. If you use a metal or plastic bow, make sure it is stiff and strong enough.

Now attach the string or nylon thread: Cut a piece of string or nylon thread about twice the length of the bow and tie one end to the bow, near the center. Secure the other end to the ground or a tree, by pulling the string or nylon thread taut.

Then add leverage. Cut a piece of wood or metal about 30cm long and attach it to the string or nylon thread, so that it hangs over the bow. The free end of the lever must be long enough to touch the ground. Add Activator. Attach a rod or stone to the lever to increase the weight and sensitivity of the activator. The activator must be positioned so that the animal, walking on the lever, activates it and triggers the trap.

Box trap

The box trap is a type of trap used for catching small wild animals such as mice, rats and foxes. It is called a "box" because the trap consists of a small metal or plastic box that has an opening in the side and a trigger mechanism inside.

How the cassette trap works is simple. The animal enters the box through the side opening to reach the bait positioned in the center of the box. When the pet touches the trigger mechanism, the door closes, and the pet is trapped inside.

The box trap is easy to operate and requires little technical skill. However, it is important to place the trap in a location where animals frequent, such as near a food source or along a path that animals use on a regular basis. Furthermore, it is important to check the trap regularly to avoid animals being trapped for too long.

Building a box trap in the wild takes a little more skill and creativity than building it using pre-existing materials. Here is a general guide on how to build a box trap using natural materials:

Necessary materials:
- Thin and flexible branches
- Dried twigs or dry leaves
- Rope or thread
- Bait (e.g., pet food or nuts)

Find a suitable area to build the trap, for example near a path frequented by animals.

Gather thin, flexible branches and twist them together to create a cassette structure. The box should be about 30 cm long, about 15 cm wide and about 10 cm high.

Use dry twigs or dry leaves to fill the box and make it more solid.

Attach a string or wire to the top of the cassette so you can lift the toggle.

Create a stalk using a thin, flexible twig, bending it to create a "U" shape with pointed ends.

Secure the lever to the base of the cassette using a string or wire, so that it hangs slightly inside the cassette.

Then you must place the bait in the center of the box.

Gently pull on the string or wire to lift the latch and secure the string or wire to the outside of the box using a small branch or other object.

Drop trap

It's a trap that uses gravity to capture the animal. The dead drop trap is a type of trap that uses a drop system to catch the wild animal. The trap consists of a cage or box placed over an opening in the ground. Inside the cage or box, bait is placed to attract the animal. Once the animal enters the cage or box and touches the bait, the drop mechanism is activated, and the animal is trapped under the weight of the cage or box.

Deadfall traps can be made in a variety of ways and from a variety of materials but are typically constructed with a wooden or metal cage or box, a rope or rope for the fall mechanism, and a rod or lever. to activate the drop. Some variants of the dead drop trap also use a spring system to increase the speed of the drop.

Here are the steps to follow to build a pitfall trap:

- Material preparation: Get a piece of wood, strong rope or wire, and a noose or cage in which to trap the animal.
- Building the frame: Create a box or cage large enough to hold the animal you want to catch. Make sure the box or cage is strong enough to support the weight of the animal.
- Preparing the drop mechanism: Secure one end of the string or wire to the center of the bottom of the box or cage. Secure the other end to a branch or lever so the rope can slide freely.
- Adding the Noose: Place a noose or trap inside the box or cage and secure it to the bottom of the box or cage so the pet cannot break free. Make sure the noose is large enough to ensnare the animal without injuring it.
- Activation of the trap: place a bait inside the box or cage to attract the animal. When the animal enters the box or cage to take the bait, the falling mechanism will activate, and the animal will be trapped.

Conibear trap

The conibear trap, also called a force trap, is a type of trap for catching wild animals. This type of trap consists of a metal spring which holds two U-shaped metal plates open, where the animal enters. When the animal activates the trap, the two metal plates forcefully close over its head or neck, killing it instantly.

The conibear trap was designed to be an instant-kill trap, thus reducing the suffering of the trapped animal. This type of trap has been used for hunting and survival for decades and is still widely used today in many countries for catching wild animals such as rodents, beavers, raccoons and other small mammals.

Here are the steps to follow to build a conibear trap:

- Choosing the type of conibear: There are several types of conibears, which vary in size and strength. It is important to choose a conibear appropriate to the size of the animal you want to catch.
- Creating the Structure: Wood or other strong materials can be used to create the structure of the trap. You will have to create a U-shaped structure, where the plates of the conibear can rest.
- Fixing the conibear: Once the structure is created, the conibear must be fixed to the top of the U, so that it can move freely.
- Create the trigger: The trigger is the part of the trap that is activated by the animal. The trigger can be created using a piece of wood or metal, attached to the bottom of the U and connected to the conibear by string or wire.
- Create the path: for the animal to enter the trap, a path must be created that leads him towards it. Baits, scents or other techniques may be used to attract the animal.
- Place the trap: finally, you will have to place the trap in the right place, where the animal usually passes.

Remember that:
- ✓ The more traps you trigger, the more likely you are to catch an animal.
- ✓ Rub the laces with dirt to remove your own odor from the traps.
- ✓ Obstruct or block the passages with branches, boulders, logs or other to divert the animals towards the traps.
- ✓ Remember where you have set the traps and check regularly (if you let the prey pass too long, it could be able to free itself or become food for other animals).
- ✓ Always make sure the trap works by testing it several times before using it.
- ✓ If you spot a herd or group of animals, you know which way it's moving, go around it and place traps in their path. Alternatively, place traps wherever you want and then try to get around the herd by going the other way. To do this, move slowly and blend in; be careful, the animals have excellent eyesight and an excellent sense of smell. Suddenly catch the herd from behind, agitate and make

noise to scare the animals trying to direct them as much as possible in the area where you have hidden the traps.

Setting traps for small game

Here are some tips on setting traps for small game:

Choosing the right location: it is important to identify the right area to place the trap. Small game mainly moves along trails, streams and other transitional areas. Try to locate these places to place traps strategically.

- Choosing the type of trap: There are different types of small game traps, such as guillotine traps, snap traps or rope traps.
- Use baits: baits are essential for attracting small game to the trap. You can use fruits, grains, seeds or insects as bait. Make sure you choose a bait suitable for the species of game you want to catch.
- Check traps regularly: It is important to check traps regularly to avoid game being trapped for too long.
- Traps for small game should be made from sturdy material, which will then be fashioned into the shape of a noose. The perfect material could be string, wire or thin rope, placed outside the animal's den or on the path usually used by the animal to move.
- The noose must be shaped in such a way that it passes through the animal's head.
- Small game traps are used in bushcraft to obtain food from the wild. Here are some examples of small game traps:
- Guillotine Trap: This trap involves the use of a sharp blade that lowers when the animal snaps the trap. The blade decapitates the animal and kills it immediately. This type of trap requires attention and care in its preparation.
- Snap Trap: This trap uses a spring that is activated when the animal snaps the trap. The spring imprisons the animal without killing it. This type of trap is less dangerous for the animal and allows the animal to be caught alive.
- Rope Trap: This trap involves the use of a rope that imprisons the animal when the trap is triggered. The rope can be wrapped around the animal's neck or its body. This type of trap is less dangerous for the animal and allows the animal to be caught alive.
- Bird Trap: Bird traps can be made in a variety of ways, but generally involve using a cage with a bait inside. The bird enters the cage to take the bait and is trapped.
- Insect Trap: Insect traps can be made in a variety of ways, but generally involve using a container with bait inside. Insects enter the container to take the bait and become trapped.

Setting traps for larger game

Creating traps for large game requires technical skills and specialized materials. Large animal traps are designed to be large and sturdy enough to catch animals such as deer, boar and bear.

Deadfall and snare have been popular trapping techniques for large game in the past but are not legal in many countries and are not considered ethical by many people due to their potential to inflict pain and suffering on animals. Instead, trapping techniques that are commonly used today include live traps, nets, and shotguns.

Living traps are designed to capture the animal without causing it harm, and the hunter can later release the animal in a safe area. Nets are used to catch birds and are made of fine threads that keep the prey from flying away. Shotguns are used to shoot animals, but only in circumstances where hunting is legal and regulated.

Furthermore, it is important to note that the hunting of large animals is often regulated by local and national laws, and hunters must obtain the necessary permits and comply with the rules established to ensure animal safety and the sustainability of the animal population.

Here are some general steps for setting up a big game trap:

- Choosing the right materials for building the trap is essential. For a large trap, it is recommended to use solid wood and strong steel wires.
- Trap Design: The trap should be designed to catch the animal safely and without causing harm. It is recommended to use a cage or cut trap to avoid harm to the animal.
- Construction of the trap: Construction of the trap requires manual dexterity and patience. In general, the trap should be large enough to hold the animal and strong enough to resist the forces of the animal when it tries to escape.
- Placement of the trap: Once the trap is built, it is important to place it in the right place. It is recommended that you hide the trap and use bait to lure the animals into the trap area.
- Trap monitoring: It is important to check the trap regularly to ensure that the trapped animal is in good condition and to avoid catching unwanted animals.

It should be remembered that large game traps are not easy to set up in the field and require some experience and knowledge to use safely and effectively. Preparing and installing traps requires attention to details, such as choosing a site to place, selecting the type of trap, and installing safety devices to prevent other animals or people from accidentally meeting the trap.

Ethical considerations in trapping

Catching animals in bushcraft can raise important ethical questions. While wildlife trapping can be an essential skill for survival in the wild, it's important to consider the effects of our actions on the environment and wildlife.

Here are some ethical considerations to keep in mind when bushcrafting animals:

- Respect for animal life: Wild animals have the right to live free and not to be captured or killed unless absolutely necessary for human survival. When trapping an animal, it is important to do it as humanely as possible to minimize the animal's suffering.
- Sustainability: When trapping wild animals, it is important to do so sustainably and responsibly. This means catching only animals you need to survive, avoiding catching endangered or endangered species, and complying with local hunting and fishing rules and laws.
- Ecosystem Impact: This means that it is important to consider the effect that the capture of an animal can have on the population of that species and on other species that depend on it for their livelihoods.
- Alternative to Trapping: In some situations, it may be possible to avoid the capture of wild animals by using other techniques, such as berry picking or line fishing. Before catching an animal, it is important to evaluate whether there are more sustainable alternatives.

PART 4: NAVIGATION AND KNOTS

Chapter 1: Navigation

The importance of navigation in the wilderness

Navigation is an essential skill in bushcraft because it allows you to navigate unfamiliar natural environments and find your way to your desired destination. Navigation can be especially important in emergencies or situations where you are lost.

Here are some of the reasons navigations is important in bushcraft:

- Orientation: Navigation allows you to determine your position and to orient yourself with respect to the desired destination. This is especially important in unfamiliar natural environments where there are no navigational cues such as roads, road signs or buildings.
- Safety: Knowing your location and the road to follow to reach your desired destination can help ensure your safety. This means that navigation is especially important in emergencies or in situations where you are lost.
- Saving time and energy: Navigation allows you to find the shortest and most efficient way to reach your desired destination. This means that navigation can help save time and energy when traveling in natural environments.

Navigation tools

Navigation is a core survival and bushcraft skill, and there are several navigational tools used by bushcraft practitioners. Here are some of the most common navigation tools in bushcraft:

Topographic map

It symbolically represents the territory in which we move, indicating paths, roads, rivers, woods, rock faces, shelters, villages. We can read the altitudes, the names of the mountains and valleys. In bushcraft, the topographic map is an important source of information about landforms, streams, forests, and other geographic features that can be used for orientation and for finding natural resources.

In bushcraft, the knowledge of reading a topographic map is therefore essential to move safely and successfully in the wild environment and to make the most of the natural resources available.

Compass

Indicates North and consequently the other cardinal points. It allows you to orient the topographic map and establish travel directions. With it, we can identify unknown points or our position, through the so-called "triangulation".

Altimeter

An altimeter is an instrument that measures the altitude of an object relative to sea level. The altimeter works by means of an atmospheric pressure measurement system. Altimeter measures barometric pressure and converts it into an altitude value.

There are several types of altimeters, such as barometric altimeters, which use a pressure capsule to measure altitude, and GPS altimeters, which use GPS signals to calculate altitude. Altimeters are often used in conjunction with topographic maps for land navigation and mountain hiking, so that you can determine your exact location and elevation relative to surrounding landmarks.

In bushcraft, the altimeter helps determine the elevation of the terrain and your location relative to landmarks such as mountains, valleys, streams, and other landscape features. This information is essential for planning your route, building shelters, and finding natural resources like water, wood, and food.

In addition, the altimeter helps prevent navigation problems and avoid dangerous situations such as climbing slopes that are too steep or descending valleys too quickly. The altimeter can also help identify landmarks along the way, such as mountain passes or valleys, which can be used for orientation and for reaching a specific destination.

The altimeter is especially useful in situations of poor visibility when it is difficult to locate landmarks and when the topographic map can be difficult to read. In these situations, the altimeter can provide a more accurate indication of your location and the elevation of the surrounding terrain.

GPS

Knowing how to navigate in any situation is essential for the bushcrafter, expert or novice. If you are a beginner, it is vitally important to proceed with the excursion only if equipped with a working GPS, able to indicate the route even in the high mountains, in the thick bush or in remote areas.

On paper, bushcraft was born as an extreme discipline, capable of catapulting the hiker into wild nature and making him rediscover the connection with it, having to provide for his own survival without using technology. As humans born and raised in civilized society, immediately thrusting ourselves into such an unvarnished experience may not be the optimal decision, as we would not be able to complete even the most basic tasks, such as orienting ourselves in a totally uncontaminated place and knowing how to find your way home.

For this reason, in addition to paper maps and the good old compass (which a hiker should be able to use with confidence) there are portable GPS, electronic devices with a precise cartographic system inside to help you find your bearings even in truly extreme situations. These portable receivers should never be missing from the bushcrafter's backpack, especially if he intends to explore new territories.

For these reasons it is highly recommended to add a good portable GPS to your selection of bushcraft accessories. These are devices created to resist extremely well in extreme situations, which are not afraid of shocks, blows, water or dirt. Their battery is very long lasting, many can last almost a full day of uninterrupted use.

There are models with a built-in cartographic system, and others that provide for the download of the maps of interest from the internet, or via SD memory. Portable GPS can be touchscreen or equipped with a hand pad, depending on the hiker's preferences. The GPS connects to specific antennas, which receive the signal even in difficult situations due to dense vegetation or altitude.

These devices, in addition to marking the route, are able to detect distances and other fundamental data on the surrounding landscape, as well as bring the hiker back safely to the starting path. It is therefore a fundamental accessory, in which it is wise to invest to ensure a pleasant and above all safe bushcraft experience.

Wristwatch

A wristwatch can be used to determine the direction of north roughly.

To use the wristwatch for orientation, hold it flat and position the hour hand towards the sun. Next, find the angle between the hour hand and the 12 o'clock on the clock and divide this angle by two. The imaginary line that is obtained, starting from the number 12 and passing through the midpoint of the corner, indicates the south direction.

In this way, it is possible to orientate oneself and determine the position of the cardinal points, even in the absence of other orientation tools such as the compass or GPS.

However, it is important to note that using the wristwatch for orientation requires some precautions. For example, it is important to use the wristwatch only when the sun is high enough in the sky, i.e., between about 9:00 and 15:00, and when the sky is clear enough. Furthermore, it must be considered that the wristwatch may not provide absolute precision in determining the cardinal points, especially in the event of adverse weather conditions or rough terrain.

How to read a map and use a compass

The definition of a geographical map can be summarized in these simple words:

An approximate, reduced and symbolic graphical representation of a part of the earth's surface on a plane, i.e., on a sheet of paper.

The maps we use in nature are topographic maps, i.e., with scales ranging from 1:10,000 to 1:100,000. All charts are oriented to the north.

The scale is the first data to take into consideration when reading a card, the greater the scale the greater the details present. The scale is the ratio between the distance measurable on the map (which will always be 1) and the real distance on the territory. So, if a topographic map has a scale of 1:25,000 it means that one centimeter on the map is equivalent to 25,000 centimeters in reality or 250 meters, the same distance measured on a map with a scale of 1: 100,000 is equivalent to 1 kilometer.

Contour lines, also called contour lines, indicate the height, expressed in meters, with respect to sea level. You will notice on the map two types of contour lines, with different thickness of the drawn stroke, namely:

- THIN LINE (called Ordinary): indicates a difference in height of 25 meters compared to the previous line.
- FAT LINE (called Directrices): indicates a difference in height of 100 meters with respect to the previous thick line.

The contour lines allow you to immediately understand the types of paths. In fact, you may find yourself in one of the following three cases:

- You walk on level ground: the stretch of path follows the level line in parallel and therefore you will walk at the same altitude, on a flat stretch.
- You walk uphill: the path crosses the contour lines perpendicularly, from a lower to a higher altitude.
- You walk downhill: the path crosses the contour lines perpendicularly, this time inversely.
- Another feature that allows you to understand, at the same distance, is the slope/steepness of the path:
- Steep section: very close contour lines.
- Simple line: contour lines with a good distance between them.

The legend, placed on the title page, groups all the symbols present on the map, they vary according to the publishing house.

You will then be able to immediately check some strategic points along or near the route such as:
- Trails
- Shelters
- Bivouacs
- Points of historical/landscape interest

They will also be very useful for you, as a reference, to orient yourself with the compass.

The topographic map is divided by a series of vertical and horizontal lines superimposed on the map. Each quadrant is represented by two numbers, placed on the edges of the map which represent the coordinates expressed in the UTM (Universal Transverse Mercator) unit of measurement.

The UTM system is the system most used in new editions of topographic maps.

The Lattice will allow you to:
- Orient the map correctly.
- Quickly locate coordinates.
- Being able to communicate your location.

How to use the compass

There are many different types of compasses on the market today, but they all serve the same purpose which is to help you find north and orient you on your hikes in nature.

Reading a compass is easy. To use a compass correctly you only need to know one thing: one end of the needle always points north. The north-pointing end of the needle is almost always red while the other side of the needle can be white, black, or some other color.

Here are some tips on how to use a compass correctly:
- Hold the compass horizontally, with the base resting on the palm of your hand and the rotating cap facing up.
- Check that the magnetic needle is free to spin and is aligned with the "N" stamped on the rotating cap. If the needle is skewed or stuck, turn the compass until the needle lines up with the "N".

- Spin the spinner cap until the magnetic needle lines up with the arrow "N" printed on the bottom of the cap.
- Read the direction that the arrow on the capsule points to. This is the direction of magnetic north.
- To determine the direction of another point, rotate your body until the direction you want to locate is in the same line of sight as the arrow on the capsule. Read the direction indicated by the graduation printed on the capsule.

In general, the compass is a very useful tool for orienting yourself outdoors, especially when walking or hiking. It is important to note that the compass locates the direction of magnetic north and not geographic. Magnetic north and true north can be different in some areas of the Earth, so be aware of the difference and consider it in your navigation.

Natural navigation methods

Natural navigation is the ability to orient and move in nature without the aid of technological tools such as a compass or GPS. The methods of natural navigation are based on the observation of natural elements such as the sun, the stars, the moon, the wind and the vegetation, and on the knowledge of the characteristics of the territory.

Orientation with the sun

The sun is the simplest and most infallible compass. The most common method of orienting yourself by the sun is solar navigation. To use this method, one must locate the shadow of an object, such as a stick or stone, and observe in which direction it falls. This direction indicates the position of the sun, and therefore the direction of the west. To locate the east direction, simply face the shade and turn 180 degrees.

Another method of orienting yourself with the sun is to use a sundial. To build a sundial, place a vertical stick on the ground and mark the time when the sun casts its shortest shadow. Subsequently, the other hours are marked, and the dots are joined to obtain a sundial. In this way, the sundial can be used to determine the position of the sun and therefore the direction.

Finally, direct observation of the sun can be used to find direction. To do this, it is necessary to observe the position of the sun with respect to the horizon, bearing in mind that the sun rises in the east and sets in the west. At midday, which is when the sun is at its highest point in the sky, it is due south.

Orientation with the moon

The moon can be a useful tool for orienting yourself in nature, especially on clear nights. Here are some ways to orient yourself by the moon:

Moon Phases: Moon phases can provide an estimate of the moon's position in the sky and therefore its direction. For example, during the full moon phase, the moon rises on the eastern horizon and sets on the western horizon, while during the new moon phase, the moon rises and sets with the sun. In general, the moon moves from east to west during the night.

Orientation by waxing or waning moon: The waxing moon appears in the east and moves west, while the waning moon appears in the west and moves east. By observing the position of the moon and comparing it with your own position, you can estimate the direction.

Elevation Angle: The elevation angle of the moon can give an indication of your position relative to the equator. For example, if the moon is high in the sky, you are near the equator, while if it is low in the sky, you are closer to the poles.

Orient yourself with the stars

Orienting yourself by the stars is one of the oldest and most widely used methods of natural navigation. Here are some tips on how to navigate by the stars:

Identifying constellations: The first thing to do is learn to recognize the most common constellations in the night sky. Some of the easiest constellations to spot are Ursa Major, Ursa Minor, Southern Cross, and Orion.

Locating the Pole Star: Once you have identified the constellations, you can look for the Pole Star, which is located near the constellation Ursa Minor. The Pole Star is useful because it is located near the North Celestial Pole and therefore provides a constant reference for navigation.

Calculate the direction: once the North Star has been identified, the position of the other stars can be used to calculate the direction. For example, if you locate Ursa Major and draw an imaginary line joining the two stars that form the "edge" of the bear, this line indicates the north-south direction.

Use Stars as a Clock: Stars can also be used as a clock to determine approximate time. For example, you can use the location of Ursa Major to calculate time based on its position relative to the horizon.

How to orient yourself with plants

Plants can be used to orient oneself in nature, in particular through the knowledge of some plant species which can provide indications on the direction or on the presence of water or other points of interest.

If we pay attention to the nature that surrounds us, we can still orient ourselves by following these tracks:

- ✓ The north-facing part of the bark of tall trees is generally covered with moss due to the higher humidity.
- ✓ On the stumps of a felled tree the growth rings are wider on the south side.
- ✓ The foliage is thickest on the south side of the tree.
- ✓ The sun melts the snow faster towards the south-facing side.
- ✓ Presence of moss on the side of the rocks facing north.
- ✓ Higher humidity in the undergrowth facing north.
- ✓ To the south there are cleaner stones and drier rocks.

Here are some tips on how to orient yourself with plants:

- Moss: Moss grows best on the north side of trees and rocks, as it is less exposed to direct sunlight and therefore more humid. By looking at the moss on a tree or rock, one can estimate the north-south direction.
- Trees: Trees can be used as reference points, especially if they are solitary or particularly large trees. By observing the shape of the tree, one can estimate the direction of the prevailing wind, which usually blows in the opposite direction to the direction of the topmost leaves.
- Sunflower: the sunflower is a plant that follows the sun during the day and orients itself towards it. By observing the position of the sunflower, the east-west direction can be estimated.
- Other Plants: Some plant species are associated with the presence of water or other points of interest. For example, glasswort grows in brackish coastal areas and shepherd's purse indicates the presence of moist soils.

How to stay on course and avoid getting lost

Knowing how to navigate is essential if you want to live in nature. Just as the use of a geographical map and compass is essential, it is equally essential, as well as useful, to know some techniques for maintaining a course (direction and towards) along the chosen path.

The direction, i.e., the ideal axis on which one moves, can be maintained when a fixed point to refer to is identified.

The first essential reference is the sun. Some rather expert and sensitive people are able to recognize the cardinal points by simply observing the position of the sun in the sky. This type of observation is all the simpler the further away you are from the equator, since the condition in which the sun is exactly at the Zenith can occur precisely at the equator (that is, on the vertical axis with respect to the person), a condition which, in the middle of a desert, makes it impossible to understand where the cardinal points are.

In this situation the only possibility to identify the cardinal points is to observe the movement of the sun which describes an arc in the sky that goes from east to west.

Once the cardinal points have been determined, a direction can be chosen. Those who are unable to identify the cardinal points using the compass or simply observing the sun can refer to the combination of sun and clock if this is equipped with hands.

This is a rather simple method: you rotate the clock until the hour hand points in the direction of the sun. The axis that divides the angle identified by the hour and minute hands in half is the North-South axis; South is positioned in the direction closest to that of the Sun.

We have also said that the use of the compass is essential in order not to lose one's orientation; however, its use can go far beyond the simple identification of one's position within a space and with the use of a geographical map.

The compass allows you to maintain your direction, i.e., the ideal axis that we have mentally traced, and which should lead us to the goal.

Getting around in nature may not be as simple as getting around the city. The presence of woods, bushes, rocks, ditches or fractures in the hills, valleys and inlets, slopes and escarpments can force us to change direction constantly and suddenly.

The change of direction during the excursion is the most delicate moment, especially if we feel uncomfortable in an unfamiliar territory. Therefore, it is good to keep a direction in a straight line, usually corresponding to the one in which our goal is located, unless we are following well-marked paths.

Once the direction line has been identified on the map, we will place the direction arrow on the compass plate parallel to it.

As we walk, we will hold the compass in our hand, taking care to keep the desired direction fixed.

Being forced to change course, a change of direction would risk making us rotate with the compass, thus losing the direction we had previously chosen.

For this reason, the best practice would be to stop at each change of direction, observe which point the direction arrow of the compass points to and, keeping it stationary in space, change one's direction. By carrying out this simple procedure of stopping and changing direction, keeping the position of the compass fixed, it is possible to maintain the direction towards the chosen objective. We can also summarize this technique by saying that it is sufficient to keep the angle formed between the direction arrow and the magnetic arrow constant.

This technique, however, is not enough to be sure of reaching a well-defined point. Any movement perpendicular to the chosen direction must be compensated for by an opposite movement. If the sum of the shifts to the right or left with respect to the direction do not compensate for each other, we will never be able to reach a precise point.

Let's take a practical example: to overcome a pit we will move perpendicularly (to the right or to the left) with respect to the chosen direction for a distance of 100 steps and then we will proceed again in the chosen direction; once we have passed the pit we will have to compensate for those hundred steps with as many steps perpendicularly to the chosen direction but in the opposite direction to that taken in the first detour.

This problem is more important the greater the deviation from the route. When we circumnavigate a trench, as in the previous example, we can easily find our correct direction. But when we have to circumnavigate a hill or a dense wooded spot, lateral movements with respect to our direction of travel can make us lose the directrix considerably.

Chapter 2: Knot-Tying and Rope Work

The importance of rope in bushcraft

Rope is one of the most important tools for bushcrafting. It is useful in many situations and can be used to build shelters, tie and drag lumber, create traps and much more. Here's why rope is so important in bushcraft:

- Shelter Building: When building shelters, rope can be used to tie the branches together and create a stable structure.
- Lumber Harvesting: The rope can be used to haul lumber or to create a pulley to lift heavy branches.
- Trap Making: Rope can be used to make traps for hunting or fishing.
- Attaching Tools: The rope can be used to secure tools such as hatchets, knives and other equipment.
- Repairs: When equipment or shelter is broken or damaged, the rope can be used to make temporary repairs.
- Safety: The rope can be used for creating seat belts, ladders and other safety devices.

The rope can also be used to create climbing ropes or to create ropes for carrying equipment.

Types of rope and cordage

There are several types of rope that can be used in bushcraft, each with their own characteristics and benefits.

Paracord

The first type of rope perfect for bushcraft is paracord. Paracord, as the name also suggests, is the string that is used to make the parachute. Consequently, it is an extremely resistant rope, tested to resist tearing and very strong stresses. In essence it is a set of thin nylon strings intertwined with a sheath that encloses them all.

The excellent quality paracord is the military type and can be recognized because inside it is composed of 7/9 filaments (one of these of a different color), composed in turn of 3 other nylon filaments.

Paracord can be used for many purposes, including fishing. Being composed of increasingly thinner threads, a line can be created by separating the thread. Another way to use the paracord is also to wrap it in the handles of some tools to greatly improve the grip.

They can also be used to mount the Tarp to build a shelter for the night or in any case for all those occasions in which we need an extremely resistant and slightly elastic rope.

Jute twine

The second most used type of rope is jute twine. Jute twine rope is a rope made from natural fibers of jute, a plant that grows mainly in India and Bangladesh. Jute twine rope is generally made up of several fibers woven together to form a single strand. This rope is often used in bushcraft for building shelters, tying down equipment, or setting traps for hunting or fishing.

Jute twine rope is relatively cheap and easy to find. It is also very strong, durable and can withstand a certain amount of weight. Jute twine rope is relatively easy to work with and handle. Being a rope made of natural fibers, it is quite soft to the touch and is pleasant to handle. Also, as you rightly said, jute twine rope holds knots well, making it ideal for many bushcraft tying tasks.

Also, the jute twine rope is generally easy to cut with a knife or scissors. This means that you can cut it into pieces of different lengths, as needed, without the need for specialized tools.

The jute twine rope is 100% biodegradable, meaning it will naturally degrade over time when exposed to the natural elements. This can be an advantage or a disadvantage depending on the circumstances. If you are using the jute twine rope for temporary tasks, such as building a temporary shelter or hunting trap, its biodegradability could be an advantage, as it saves you having to collect the cut pieces once you are finished. activity. On the other hand, if you are using jute twine rope for a long-term project, such as a permanent construction job, its biodegradability could be a disadvantage. In this case, it may be preferable to use a stronger and more durable synthetic rope that can withstand harsh weather and conditions for a longer period.

Jute rope may be less resistant to water and moisture than other ropes, such as nylon or polypropylene rope. Additionally, jute rope can be more susceptible to wear and tear than other synthetic ropes.

In general, jute twine rope is a good choice for bushcraft activities that require moderate use of the rope in dry weather conditions. However, if you plan to use the rope in wet or rainy conditions, or to lift very heavy objects, it may be preferable to choose a synthetic rope that is more resistant to water and wear.

The sisal rope

Sisal rope is a rope made from natural fibers obtained from the sisal plant, a plant native to Mexico but also grown in other parts of the world. Sisal rope is often used in bushcraft to build shelters, tie down equipment, or for setting traps for hunting or fishing. Sisal rope is relatively cheap and easy to find, and it is also strong and durable, making it suitable for many bushcraft activities. Additionally, sisal rope is resistant to decay and harsh weather conditions, making it a popular choice for outdoor activities.

However, sisal rope also has some limitations. For example, sisal rope may be less resistant to wear and tear than other synthetic ropes, such as nylon or polypropylene rope. Additionally, sisal rope may be less resistant to water and moisture than other ropes, which may make it less suitable for bushcrafting in wet or rainy environments.

Unlike jute twine rope, sisal rope has a rougher texture and may feel less soft to the touch. This could make it less comfortable to handle, especially if you're using it for long-lasting activities or dealing with a significant amount of friction.

However, there are some tricks to making sisal rope softer and easier to handle. For example, rope can be softened by soaking it in hot water and letting it air dry. Alternatively, a fabric softener solution can be applied to the rope to make it softer to the touch.

Also, when sisal rope gets wet and dry, it tends to hold its original shape, which can make it more difficult to undo the knots. This could be a problem if you use sisal rope for tasks that require you to tie and untie knots frequently, such as building temporary shelters. However, this aspect of sisal rope could also be considered an advantage in some situations. For example, if you are using sisal rope to tie down equipment or items that need to stay put, its ability to hold its original shape could be helpful in ensuring that the binding remains stable and does not come loose.

In general, sisal rope is a common choice for many bushcraft activities due to its durability and strength, but it is important to consider the environmental conditions in which it will be used and its limitations compared to other synthetic ropes.

Propylene rope

Polypropylene rope, also known as polypropylene rope, is a synthetic rope commonly used in bushcraft. It is made from a water, UV and chemical resistant polypropylene fiber, making it strong and durable. One of the main characteristics of the polypropylene rope is its flexibility. Thanks to its elasticity, the polypropylene rope can be easily knotted and untied, making it very versatile for a wide range of bushcraft activities, such as building temporary shelters, climbing, or retrieving objects.

Additionally, polypropylene rope is lightweight and easy to carry, making it a great choice for hikers and campers who want to keep the weight of their gear to a minimum.

This means it may be less suitable for activities involving high friction or requiring increased wear resistance. In addition, polypropylene rope can be subjected to even permanent deformation due to its elasticity, which could limit its usefulness in some bushcraft activities.

Kevlar rope

Kevlar rope is a synthetic rope that uses a synthetic fiber called "aramid", commercially known as Kevlar, as the base material. Kevlar is a strong and durable synthetic material that is often used in industrial and military applications, such as soldier helmets, body armor and armored vehicles.

Kevlar rope exhibits a few unique properties, including high wear resistance, low stretch, and exceptional tensile and breaking strength. These properties make Kevlar rope ideal for a wide variety of bushcraft applications, such as suspension bridge building, climbing or hauling heavy objects.

Additionally, Kevlar rope has low stretch, which means it stays taut and stable even under heavy loads. This makes it particularly useful in situations where a stable and resistant binding is required.

These properties make Kevlar rope ideal for bushcraft activities in harsh environments and extreme conditions. For example, Kevlar rope is often used in marine or mountain environments where temperatures can be very low, or weather conditions can be unpredictable. Additionally, Kevlar's fire resistance can be useful in situations where there is a risk of fire, such as when working with sharp tools and heat sources. However, it is important to note that Kevlar rope is not completely flame retardant and can still burn when exposed to extremely high temperatures or for an extended period.

However, Kevlar rope also has some limitations. For example, due to its low stretch, it can be more difficult to tie and untie knots than other synthetic ropes such as propylene rope. Additionally, Kevlar rope is generally more expensive than other synthetic ropes, making it less affordable for some people.

White line rope

White line rope is a type of synthetic rope that is used for a variety of applications including bushcraft. This string is called the "white line" due to its color, which is usually white or beige.

The white line rope is generally made of nylon or polyester, two strong and durable synthetic materials. These materials give the rope good tensile and breaking strength as well as good weather and abrasion resistance.

It is often used in bushcraft for activities such as building shelters, climbing, lifting heavy objects and for building suspension bridges. The rope is easy to handle and knot, making it suitable for even the simplest tying tasks.

Basic knots

There are several basic knots that are important to bushcraft. Here is a list of the ones you absolutely need to know:

Slipped Overhand knot

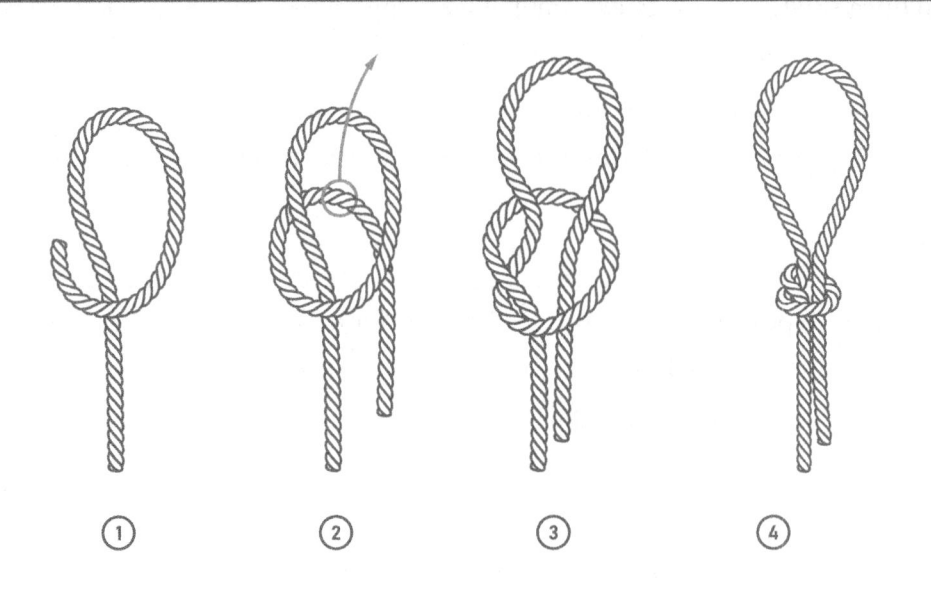

The Overhand Knot, also called a stopper knot or overhand knot, is one of the most common basic knots. It is a very simple knot, which consists of a simple turn in the rope and a passage of the lace through itself. It is mostly used as a stopper knot, to keep a rope from fraying, or to create a block shape on a rope.

The Overhand Knot can be used to secure smaller items, such as tying two threads together or locking the end of a rope to prevent it from fraying. However, for heavier objects or situations that require greater security, it is recommended to use more complex and secure knots.

In general, the Overhand Knot is a versatile and useful knot to know, especially for bushcraft beginners. With practice, you can use this knot in many common situations and also create more complex variations like the Overhand Bend or Overhand Loop.

The overhand knot is very easy to make and works well with any type of rope or thread. However, it is important to note that the overhand knot is not the safest and most reliable knot when dealing with heavy loads or situations where safety is a priority. In these cases, it is necessary to use more complex and secure knots, such as the boatman's knot or the half-boatman's knot.

The Overhand Knot is a very simple and quick knot to tie. Follow the steps below to create it:

- Take one end of the string and fold it over itself to create a loop.
- Thread the end of the string through the loop.
- Pull the two opposite ends of the string in opposite directions to tighten the knot.

Timber Hitch Knot

A timber hitch knot, also known as a quick hitch knot, is a knot used to secure rope to a post or tree trunk. It's a simple but very effective knot to secure the rope in place quickly and securely.

To run the Quick Hitch Knot, follow these steps:

- Loop the rope around the post or tree trunk and tie a basic knot, such as a bear loop or slipknot.
- Tie a half knot over the previous round, bringing the string under and then over the round.
- Tie a second half-knot over the first one, bringing the string under and then over the previous round.
- Thread the string through the spaces between the two half knots and the previous round.
- Pull the rope hard to tighten the Snag hitch.

Half Hitch Knot

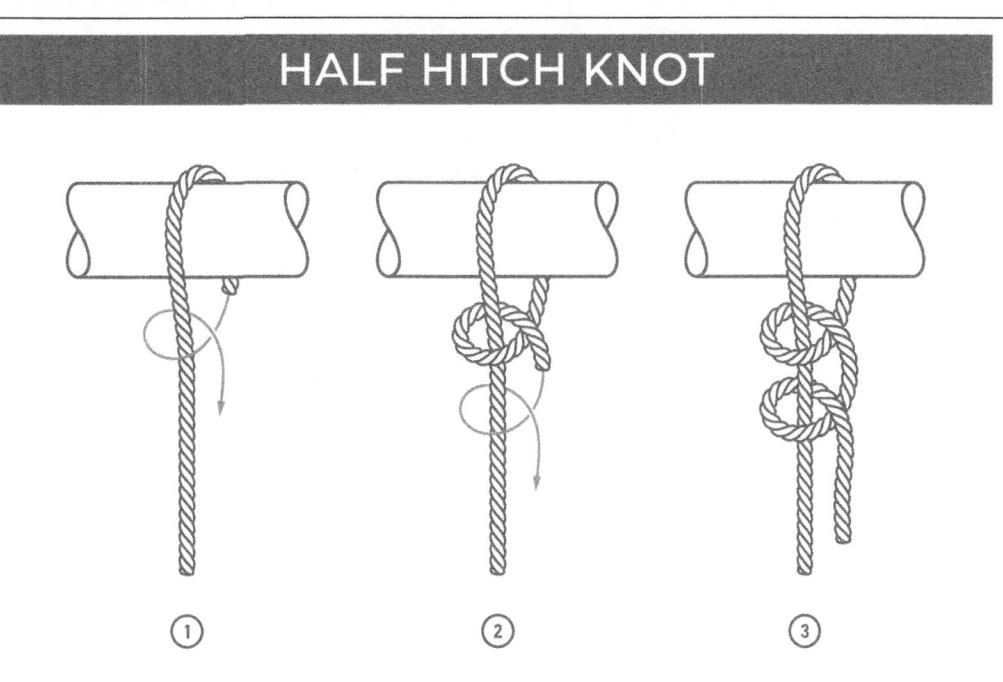

The half hitch knot, also known as a "half boatman", is a type of knot used to temporarily block a rope. It is a very simple knot to make: just fold the rope on itself and tie a simple knot inside the fold, in order to create a knot that blocks the rope. The half hitch knot is often used in situations where a rope needs to be temporarily blocked, such as to secure a tent or tarp. It is important to note that the half hitch knot is not a self-locking knot; therefore, it may become loose when subjected to strong traction. For this reason, it is always important to check that the knot is tight before using the blocked rope.

The half hitch knot is not particularly strong and can come loose under heavy pulling. Also, the knot can become difficult to undo if it has been put under a lot of tension. For this reason, the half hitch knot is often used only as a preliminary step to creating other more complex knots, such as the full hitch knot or figure eight.

Here's how you can make the half hitch knot:

- Take the string and wrap it around the rod or object you want to tie it to.

- Take the end of the string and wrap one more loop around the rod or object, overlapping the first loop.
- Take the end of the rope and thread it under the second loop of rope and then over the first loop.
- Finally, pass the end of the rope through the gap between the first and second turn of rope and pull down to tighten the knot.

Advanced knots

Here is a list of the advanced level nodes you need to know:

Double Fisherman's Knot

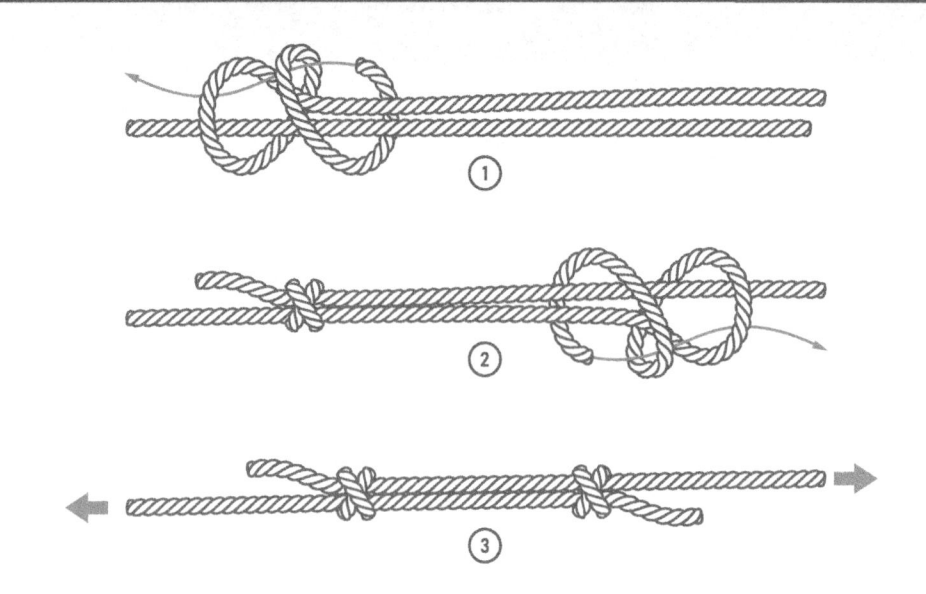

The Double fisherman's knot, also known as the double knot or the figure-of-eight knot, is a very common knot in bushcraft and fishing. The fisherman's knot, also known as a double knot, is a binding knot that is used to join two ropes together. There are several variations of the fisherman's knot, but all involve knotting two ropes to create a secure and strong bond. The fisherman's knot is often used in situations where pulling power is important, such as when climbing or towing a vehicle. Its main feature is that it maintains good resistance even when subjected to tension, without slipping or loosening.

To tie the fisherman's knot, follow these steps:

- Take the two ropes and overlap them by about 15-20cm.
- Take the end of the first string and loop it around the other string, pulling it back and then back to the front.
- Thread the end of the first string through the loop you just created.

- Now take the end of the second string and make the same turn around the first string, bringing it back and then back to the front.
- Thread the end of the second string through the loop you just created.
- Pull the two ropes slowly to tighten the knot.
- The fisherman's knot is a very strong and reliable knot, but it can be difficult to untie if it has been put under great strain. It is also important to note that the fisherman's knot reduces the strength of the rope by approximately 20%, so it is important to use it only when you need to join two ropes or create a double layer rope.

Clove Hitch Knot

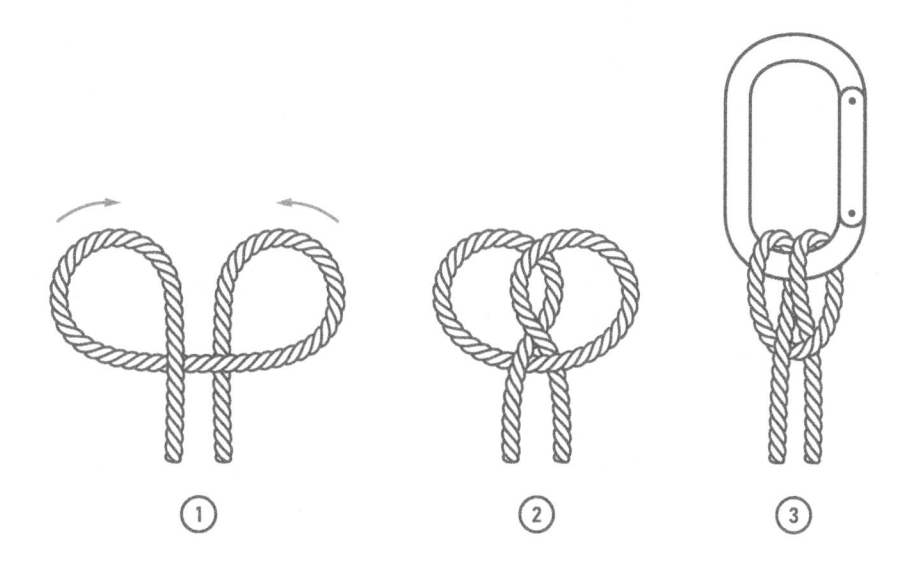

The clove knot is an anchoring knot widely used in bushcraft and other outdoor pursuits. It is created by passing the string around a post, rock or other object and then making a double loop on the same string. In this way, a secure and reliable knot is formed which keeps the object in place. It can be used effectively to climb over or around objects such as a tree trunk or pole, due to its ability to wrap the rope tightly around the anchoring object. For example, let's imagine that we have to cross a stream using a rope stretched between two trees. The clove knot can be used to secure the rope to the starting mast and then pass the rope around the finishing mast, before looping it back to the starting point. In this way, the rope tightly wraps around the arrival mast, allowing us to cross the stream safely.

The clove knot is very useful in situations where you need to anchor a rope or wire to an object, such as creating an anchor for a tent or securing a load to the top of a vehicle.

Additionally, the clove knot can be easily unlocked and removed once the rope is no longer needed, by simply pulling one end of the rope.

Here's how you can make the Clove Hitch Knot:
- Start by taking one end of the rope and place it against a post or pole so that the rope is parallel to its surface.
- Wrap the string around the post to create a vault.
- Bring the rope under the vault you created and then wrap it around the post again, creating a second loop of rope parallel to the first.
- Thread the string over the second turn of string and under the first, then feed the string through the gap between the two turns of string.
- Pull on opposite ends of the rope to tighten the knot against the post.

The Carrick Knot

SHEET BEND

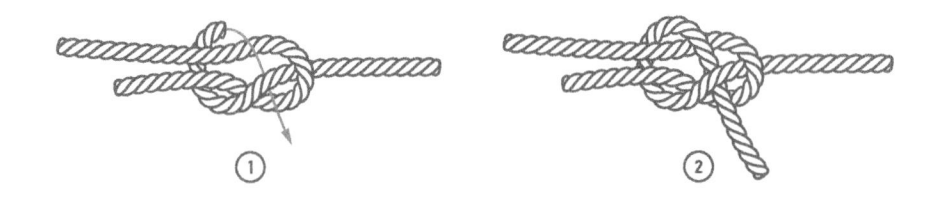

The Carrick Knot is a very useful knot in many bushcraft applications, such as building shelters or organizing gear. The Carrick knot is a knot used to join two ropes together. Its resistance does not fail even if subjected to significant traction or if immersed in water. The beautiful shape has made the Carrick knot a popular ornamental knot.

Here's how you can make it:
- Take one end of the string and loop it over the other end to create a loop. The length of the string depends on the specific needs of your application, so make sure you cut enough length.
- Take the left end of the string and loop it under the loop, then loop it over the right end of the string.
- Take the right end of the string and pull it over the bend, then pull it under the left end of the string.
- Take the left end of the string and pull it under the bight again, but this time pull it under the right end of the string as well.
- Take the right end of the string and pull it over the bend again, but this time pull it over the left end of the string as well.

- Pull the two ends of the rope in opposite directions to tighten the Carrick Knot. This knot can be further improved by adding a second turn to increase its strength and stability.
- Your Carrick Bushcraft Node is now complete! You can use it to secure equipment or build shelters in the wild. Remember that this knot takes practice to become proficient at, so practice often to become an expert.

Prusik's knot

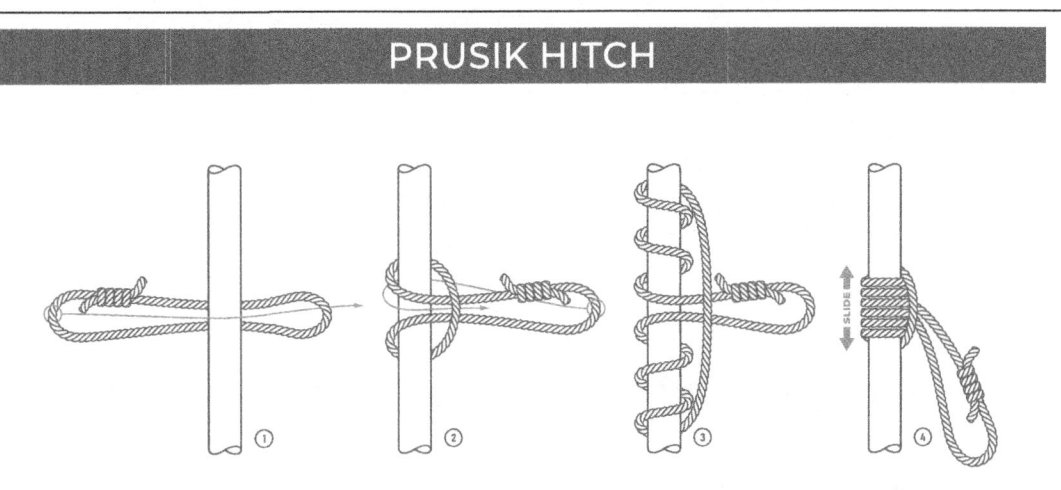

The Prusik knot is a very useful knot in bushcraft, as it allows you to create a secure connection between two ropes of different diameters, such as between a climbing rope and a branch or tree. The Prusik is a bidirectional self-locking knot, i.e. it locks with traction from both above and below and requires a minimum of experience for its execution. In addition to abseiling, it is also used for static rope ascents and rescue operations. Its blocking effect is so powerful that it is more difficult to loosen it once it is subjected to tension by the weight of our body but, precisely for this reason, it is the one with the safest grip.

Here's how to make the Prusik knot:
- Take the thinnest string (called a "string") and make a loop with one end.
- Thread the ring over the thicker string (called the "main string") and then thread the ring through itself, forming a kind of "8".
- Loop the loop over the main string a second time, sliding it under the first time.
- Grab the end of the string that sticks out of the ring and pull down, so that the knot is tightened around the main string.
- Repeat the process to create a second Prusik knot about 15-20cm away from the first so that the two knots can be used together to create a safety system.

The Prusik knot is very useful for creating a solid anchor on a main rope, for example for building a suspension bridge or climbing a tree. However, it is important to note that the knot can only slide along the main rope in one direction, so it must be positioned correctly to prevent it from shifting during use.

The bowline knot

BOWLINE KNOT

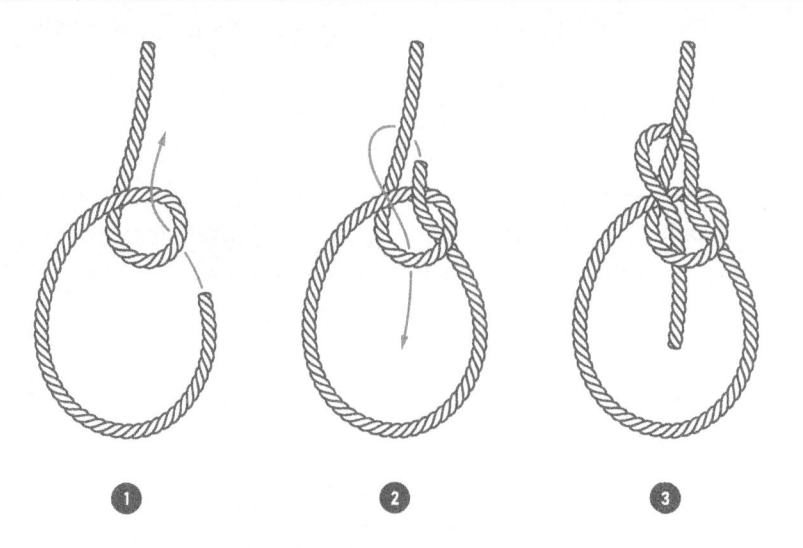

① ② ③

The double bowline knot is a very useful knot in bushcraft, as it allows you to create a solid and secure loop on the tip of a rope.

Here's how to tie the double bowline knot:

- Start by creating a loop at the tip of the string, folding the string over itself to form a loop. The part going down will become the "tail" of the knot.
- Take the tail of the string and pass it over the loop, then under the main string, and finally over the loop again.
- Pass the tail through the second loop, the one created above the main string, from bottom to top.
- Pulling on the tail of the rope, tighten the knot.
- Repeat the process to create a second double bowline knot about 15-20cm away from the first, so that the two knots can be used together to create a security system.
- The double bowline knot is very useful for creating a solid and secure loop at the end of a rope, for example to attach a rope to a tree, to create a slingshot or to build a shelter. However, it is important to note that the knot can become difficult to untie if loaded over the long term, so it is advisable to only use the knot when necessary.

How to make rope from natural materials

To make rope from natural materials, you need some materials gathered from nature, such as:
Vegetable fibers: for example, tree bark, leaves, roots, coir, grass or hemp.
There are several plants that you can use to make natural ropes, but the choice depends on the availability of these plants in your area and their properties. Here are some plants that are commonly used to make ropes:

- Tree Bark: The inner bark of some trees such as linden, pine, willow, and poplar are often used to make rope, as the bark contains long, strong fibers.
- Palm Leaves: Palm leaves, such as those of the coconut palm, can be used to make rope, as their fibers are strong and resistant to moisture.
- Coconut fibers: Coconut fibers, obtained from the peel of the fruit of the coconut palm, are very strong and resistant, but require careful processing to be used as a material for ropes.
- Grass: Some varieties of grass, such as common reed or wild flax, can be used to make rope, but they are usually less durable than other plants.
- Roots: Some roots, such as those of the rush plant, can be used to make rope, but are generally less strong than other plants.
- Other Plants: Other plants that can be used to make rope include hemp, sisal, jute and ramie.

Remember that the choice of plants to produce ropes depends on the properties of the plant, the availability of these plants in your area and the processing techniques you know. In any case, always make sure you choose healthy plants and avoid damaging the surrounding ecosystem.
The best part of the bark for making rope is the inner bark, which contains long, strong fibers. In general, plants with smooth and easily separable bark are the most suitable for the production of rope, since the bark can be easily removed, and the fibers can be obtained without damaging the underlying plant tissue.

- ✓ Stem fibers. These fibers are very long and quite strong. While not as strong or long as bark fibers, these fibers are easier to find and harvest, and consequently easier to use.
- ✓ Grass fibers. They are very short but just as strong. Grass fibers are very easy to work with, so they are a great choice if you need to make rope very quickly.

To make rope you must first separate the fibers from the plant. In general, there are three main methods of separating fibers from plants:
- Scraping: With this method, a sharp tool is used to scrape off the bark or outside of the stem of the plant, leaving the fibers inside exposed. This method is suitable for plants such as birch and linden, which have an outer bark that can be removed easily.

- Breaking: In this method, the stem of the plant is broken into small pieces and beaten with a hammer or ax to separate the fibers. This method is suitable for plants such as hemp and flax, which have elongated fibers inside the stem.
- Maceration: In this method, you soak the plant parts in water for a period so that the fibers can soften and separate from the rest of the plant. After separating the fibers from the plant, it is necessary to clean and comb them to remove any impurities and filaments. Afterwards, the fibers can be twisted or woven together to create a strong rope.

After extracting the fibers from the plant, it is important to clean and polish them to remove any impurities and make them smoother and more uniform. This process is called fiber polishing. After polishing, the fibers should be uniform, smooth and ready to be braided or woven together to create a strong rope. Divide the fibers into thin strips about 1 cm wide.

Hold three parallel strips together at the base and braid them, tying a knot at the end. Continue to weave the fibers together, being careful to keep the tension constant and applying pressure to make sure the fibers are snug together.

When you reach the end of a strip of fiber, join a new strip of fiber by intertwining it with the first one. Continue braiding the fibers together until the rope reaches the desired length.

Tie a knot at the opposite end of the rope to keep it from fraying.

PART 5: CAMP CRAFT AND FIRST AID CRASH COURSE

Chapter 1: Toolmaking and Camp Crafts

This chapter will cover the importance of tools in bushcraft, basic and advanced tool-making methods, and how to maintain and care for your tools. It will also cover camp crafts like containers, baskets and so on.

The importance of tools in bushcraft

Are you about to enter the wild and mysterious world of bushcraft and want more information on the accessories and equipment you will need to live in the name of adventure? So, we will show you a complete guide on the topic! Know that to carry out this type of activity, having the right tools is vital. To give a practical example, choosing a suitable knife for bushcraft is of fundamental importance, it is our main work tool and must be chosen with extreme care.

But so are all the others to ensure survival in the woods.

In fact, survival and bushcraft equipment is indispensable in emergency situations.

But what to bring before embarking on the next adventure is a personal matter. Do you want to go back to basics, or do you prefer to carry items with you that make the adventure or excursion a little more comfortable? Does your equipment need to be light or is weight and size not an issue? Regardless of your needs, the perfect equipment is the best way forward in this adventure.

Preparation, as well as equipment is key when you enter the world.

The right tools will make your journey on one hand much more comfortable, on the other these tools will provide to your safety. For example, carry a survival kit with essential items such as a fire starter, water filter, compass, paracord and many other things you might need during an emergency situation.

Therefore, we have made all this speech to say that, when we talk about the importance of tools, we are referring to the fundamental ones to start doing Bushcraft. And

Bushcraft, as we have already repeated during this guide, is an activity which, based on one's own experiences and style, but above all involves the use of infinite tools, all functional and useful. Obviously, there is another thing to say: the prices for the equipment can vary greatly according to the brand and the type of adventure we have to face.

There are, for example, sleeping bags designed to be used in extremely cold temperatures ranging from -68 to -122 degrees Fahrenheit and which can cost up to 1200 dollars.

Basic toolmaking

With this paragraph we want to show you the basic tools to get started without an exaggerated investment but which at the same time allows you to have everything you need for your first adventure. Are you ready? Let's start!

The basics

The first thing you need to know are the five C's or these:

1. Cutting tools
2. Cover elements
3. Combustion devices
4. Containers
5. Cordage

You will need the cutting tools to cut trees, food, branches, ropes, cloths, fabrics, etc... The covering elements (sleeping bag, towels, thermal blankets, etc...) are primarily used to create a shelter, if you stay there for a long time Combustion devices can be used to light a fire both to keep warm and to cook food, but also to create natural medicines. The containers should not be underestimated because they can be used in various cases such as collecting rainwater and then filtering it or boiling it to be drunk, or they can also be used to transport water from places far from the camp.

Finally, the rope can be used to create a shelter or to make traps but also other things.

Cutting tools (axe, utility knife, hacksaw, knife.)

Ax

The ax is a very useful tool because it can be used for various purposes: it can be used to cut down large trees, but also small ones (but it is quite inconvenient as a hacksaw or a bow saw can be used). Additionally, the ax can also be used to drive stakes into the ground using the back of the ax head. The ax is also useful for splitting wood for a fire.

As we told you, based on the type of adventure you have decided to carry out, you must prepare the right equipment, but it is essential to have a list of basic equipment that makes sure you have taken everything strictly necessary.

This is a list that works for 99% of situations:

- ✓ Knife (possibly fixed blade also called Full Tang)
- ✓ Folding saw
- ✓ Flintlock (also called Fire Steel)
- ✓ Lighter and/or windproof matches

- ✓ Water bottle + mess tin
- ✓ Rope (possibly Paracord)
- ✓ Head torch
- ✓ Waterproof poncho
- ✓ Sleeping bag
- ✓ Tarp or Tent

Bags and backpacks

Let's start with the basics of what you need to carry your equipment or backpacks and bushcraft bags with you Having a survival kit can make the bushcraft experience easier to manage, but in order to carry all the items you need to have a backpack or bag that can contain them and make them available when needed. There are many bags on the market designed for bushcraft. But for what reasons do these accessories differ from the others in common use?

Bushcraft backpacks are designed to be easily transportable, but at the same time they must guarantee excellent resistance. Bumps and unexpected events are always around the corner! Usually, these models are equipped with many pockets. Each of them is used for a precise task, without creating confusion. Thus, even in the most critical moments, you will always know exactly where a particular object is kept. Bushcraft bags vary in materials, sizes and the purpose for which they are made there are some backpacks with a maximum capacity of 30 liters, while some bags tolerate more than 50 liters. These accessories are made so that the weight is distributed over the whole body and not just on the back, and they can have an internal frame that allows you to adjust the load.

Food and water: everything you need to feed yourself.

Water and food will allow you to keep alive and will allow you to benefit from the energy needed to continue this extreme experience.

Look for water to make drinkable

Water is the resource that keeps us alive and must absolutely be found and made drinkable within a maximum period of 24 hours. Without food, it is possible to survive for a few days, but without water, dehydration occurs, and death occurs in a rather short time. In some places finding water will not be a problem since streams and waterways abound in some natural oases, but obviously it will not be possible to drink it before having subjected it to a purification process.

In fact, the water in question could be rich in dangerous bacteria which, if ingested, could trigger serious health problems, such as infections, diseases, salmonella and many other annoying and dangerous ailments. To make the water drinkable, it is possible to create natural filters capable of retaining the largest impurities, which will be used for several days to be more effective.

To create these filters, materials such as gravel, coal and sand are indicated to be placed in sheets or leaves. And remember never, ever drink stagnant water – or one that is full of bubbles or foam – as it could seriously damage your health.

Based on this list, I will now show you exactly the best products for various price ranges, you will be able to choose what to start with based on your availability.

Knife

The knife is our number one ally, but if we don't know how to use it well, it can easily become our worst enemy, causing us even very serious and difficult to heal wounds if we are in remote environments.

That said, each knife is better than another depending on the main use we have to make of it.

Below are some of our favorite knives that fall into the bushcraft category.

They are all knives of excellent workmanship and can be used for any type of outdoor activity.

Before we get into the details of our favorite knives, let's look at what makes a Bushcraft knife slightly different from other types of knives.

So, we will list the ones we consider the best:

- Overall Best Pick: Benchmade Bushcrafter
- Best Value: Morakniv Ft11742
- Budget friendly: Schrade SCHF36
- Budget Friendly: Condor Bushlore Knife

But what is the difference between a Bushcraft Knife and a Survival Knife?

Bushcraft knives differ from survival and pocketknives. Each of them has different uses which we will cover in a little detail below.

1. Survival Knives: Survival knives typically have a fixed blade and are a good option for all those who want to use them to do "anything", replacing "as far as possible" even the use of a hatchet.
2. Pocket Knives: these kinds normally are folding knives that you have always with yourself that are small and can be employed for different tasks.
3. Bushcraft Knives: A Bushcraft knife, which we discuss here, should be considered primarily a woodcutting tool and can be used effectively for carving, feathering, and creating stitches on wooden objects. Typically, not resembling a tactical knife, it should have a blade that is 3 to 6 inches long and extremely sharp. Bushcraft knives should be full tang and fixed tang knives. Like survival knives, they typically have handles that vary in material. Handle materials can include wood, micarta, and dense rubber or a rigid plastic.

When choosing a bushcraft knife you should avoid blades longer than 6 inches and start considering a machete or ax for heavy cuts.

Types of Knife Steel

They could be considered alike to the steels available for the other kinds of knives.

Anyway, the main kinds of steel you will work with for a bushcraft knife will be carbon steel and stainless steel.

For a deeper look here is a basic summary:

- ✓ High Carbon Content: HC steel will hold an edge longer but will rust more quickly. It is also softer and makes sharpening easier. If there is something to remind is to oil the blade consistently to maintain it rust-free if you live in a humid climate. Recommended high carbon steels are: 1000 Series (1045, 1095, etc.), 5160, O1, O6, W2
- ✓ Stainless Steel: SS requires more sharpening but is unlikely to rust. It usually requires less maintenance, but it's not too sharp either. Recommended stainless steels are: 400 Series (420, 440A/B/C), AUS Series (AUS-6/8/10), BG42, Bohler, S30V, VG10

But which Steel is Best for a Bushcraft Knife?

This is a very frequent question, and we will provide you a proper answer.

High Carbon is great, but if you're looking for a "one" knife that does it all, stainless steel is a better choice. We still recommend a multi-knife approach (look at them as tools suited to specific jobs).

9 of the Best Bushcraft Knives Based on Price:

Benchmade Bushcrafter Knife

Benchmade is famous for quality. They make some of the best outdoor/survival knives on the market today and the Bushcrafter is undoubtedly among them.

Here are the specs for the Benchmade Bushcrafter:

- ✓ Total length: 9.2 inches
- ✓ Blade length: 4.43 inches
- ✓ Blade Type: Drop Point
- ✓ Blade material: S30V stainless steel
- ✓ Rockwell hardness: 58-60HRC
- ✓ Handle material: G-10 plastic
- ✓ Weight: 7.72 oz.

On Amazon it has a rating of 4.8 out of 5 with 208 votes. This knife is an extremely professional tool for the competent Bushcrafter. S30V steel has a longer, stronger edge and requires much less care and maintenance than a carbon steel blade.

It is a real field knife, not a show knife to be kept in a climate-controlled casing to prevent rust. There is no need to constantly clean and oil it or worry about rain, snow, dew, blood or sap corroding the blade.

You can use it all day long, wipe it on the tail of your shirt or pant leg and go ahead, the blade will stay sharp and rust free.

The Bushcrafter features a blade made of S30V stainless steel which has inside of it 1.45% carbon and is one of the best steels for knives.

Condor Knife & Tool Bushlore

Condor Knife & Tool makes some quality knives for people on a budget.

Here are the specs:
- Total length: 9.5 inches
- Blade length: 4.375
- Blade Type: Drop Point
- Blade material: 1075 stainless steel
- Rockwell Hardness: Unknown
- Handle material: wood
- Weight: 12 oz.

The CKT Bushlore represent a great choice for a bushcraft knife and its very simple design makes it one of the most famous knives on the market. In most cases you can choose it if you're searching for a budget-friendly tool.

This knife is also great for chopping wood and creating carvings. They also make a smaller version with a 3-inch blade.

Buck Knives Bu853brs

No comparison list would be complete without listing a Buck. The Buck 853 is a great bushcraft knife at an affordable price.

Here are the specs of the Buck:
- Total length: 9.5 inches
- Blade length: 4.625 inches
- Blade Type: Drop Point
- Blade material: 420HC
- Handle material: micarta
- Weight: 181 g

While most Buck knives are American made, this one is made overseas, which helps keep the price lower than entry-level knives.

Pricewise, this knife can usually be had for under $90.00 when there are discounts on Amazon, making it a good option for anyone looking in that price range and looking to expand their collection. of knives. The handle of the knife is made of flat steel at the end, making it usable as a hammer.

Spyderco G-10 Bushcraft Knife

It's hard not to love everything about the Spyderco Bushcraft Knife. We are fans of Spyderco.

Spyderco-G-10-Bushcraft-Knife

Here are the specs:

- ✓ Length: 8.75 inches
- ✓ Blade length: 4 inches
- ✓ Blade Type: Drop Point
- ✓ Blade material: O-1
- ✓ Rockwell Hardness: Unknown
- ✓ Handle material: G-10 plastic
- ✓ Weight: 7.75 oz.

The Spyderco Bushcraft Knife is a collaboration between Tactical Bushcrafter, Chris Claycombe, BushcraftUK.com and Spyderco. They set out to create a blade that could rival some of their fixed blade competitors in terms of quality and usability.

In Bushcraft he oversees cutting and slicing. The knife comes standard with a form fitting sheath making it easy to carry right out of the box. The blade is fully interlocking which is different from most of Spyder Co's more popular offerings which are more modern pocketknives.

Tops Brothers of Bushcraft

One of the best for Bushcraft and the price tag reflects that. This knife has a few extra features that we'll talk about next, but let's look at the specs first.

Here are the specifications of the Tops BOB Knife:

- ✓ Overall length: 10 inches
- ✓ Blade length: 4.5 inches
- ✓ Blade Type: Drop Point
- ✓ Blade material: 1095HC
- ✓ Rockwell Hardness: 56-58RC
- ✓ Handle material: micarta
- ✓ Weight: 9.6 oz.

The one thing we don't love about TOPS BOB is the price tag. That said, this knife is worth considering if you're already looking at our top-quality pick which is the Benchmade Bushcrafter. The extra weight behind the BOB Fieldcraft Knife is excellent and helps make it a very effective cutting tool. While the knife already has good features, let's take a look at what has been added to make the BOB stand out.

The handle features a drilled divot that has been specially designed for fire starting. The pommel of the blade is the tang, simply wrapped around the knife handles. The thumb area is also shaped to provide a better grip when performing other tasks such as skinning or setting traps. Overall, if you can afford it, the BOB is a great choice to make sure you can't go wrong.

Morakniv Carbon Black Tactical Bushcraft Knife

Morakniv is a budget knife maker (it a $70.00 knife) .

Here are the Morakniv specs:

- ✓ Length: 9.1 inches
- ✓ Blade length: 4.3 inches
- ✓ Blade Type: Drop Point
- ✓ Blade material: HC / tungsten
- ✓ Rockwell Hardness: Unknown
- ✓ Handle material: molded rubber
- ✓ Weight: 5.7 Oz (with sheath)

Morakniv is now synonymous with quality, they are very renowned for their quality/price ratio and this knife exceeds the manufacturer's expectations. The product best reflects all that can be expected in terms of sturdiness and cutting capacity with a very sharp blade and a very angular and squared back suitable for the use of the flintlock. An excellent Bushcraft knife that on Amazon has obtained an average of 4.5 out of 5 with 612 votes.

In our opinion, Morakniv knives are unrivaled in this price range and the Mora Bushcraft Survival is a prime example of this.

It is certainly more expensive than other Moraes, due to the increased size of the blade, the peculiarities of the scabbard and perhaps also a little for a marketing question, but the value for money remains unbeatable. Versatile, robust, well designed, well-made knife, with useful options and also aesthetically beautiful.

HANDLE

Handle made by injection of a polymer with high grip power, which guarantees a secure grip even with wet hands or in the presence of dust and sand.

In the hand, the knife gives a sensation of solidity, the weight is contained but well balanced, the grip is firm and guarantees good control both in the coarser operations and in those of greater precision.

SHEATH

Made of polymer, it is resistant and not bulky.

The retention of the blade is good and should prevent accidental unsheathing. You can find a drainage hole at the knife bottom.

In conclusion we think it is excellent as equipment for bushcraft enthusiasts. We also see it well as a "school" knife for those who have their first experiences and want to learn how to handle these tools for activities in the woods.

Ontario Sk-5 Blackbird

The Ontario SK-5 Blackbird is a solid knife with a unique design. It is a blade that serves not only as a knife but as a utility tool that can be attached to a staff and used as a spear. It fits our criteria well, and we like the features the SK-5 offers.

Here are the Ontario RTAK II specs:
- ✓ Total length: 10.0 inches
- ✓ Blade length: 5.0 inches
- ✓ Blade type: spear point
- ✓ Blade material: 154 CM stainless steel
- ✓ Rockwell Hardness: Unknown
- ✓ Handle material: G10
- ✓ Weight: 12 oz.

The blade is composed of 154 CM American stainless steel. While the tang is thinner than some of the other knives on the list, the steel feels very sturdy. The handle is a G10 Plastic which gives a good grip on the handle.

We like the workmanship of the blade that has been done, as the knife feels like a quality knife, which is what OKT is known for. The sheath is a fabric material that is brown and has a somewhat tactical feel.

Helle Utvaer

A well-made knife. Robust and functional. It sets no limits for buschcraft.

Here are Helle Utvaer's specs:
- ✓ Length: 11 inches
- ✓ Blade length: 3.93 inches
- ✓ Blade Type: Drop Point
- ✓ Blade material: 12C27 stainless
- ✓ Rockwell Hardness: Unknown
- ✓ Handle material: wood
- ✓ Weight: 5.64 oz.

We personally own a dozen Helle knives. This is our favourite. Excellent balance and strength. A knife that cannot be missing from your belt. It is not so cheap, but worth it. An excellent knife. In a nutshell, the experience with Helle Utvaer was and still is one of the best.

To wrap up the talk about knives, finding the best bushcraft knife can be difficult because so many people have different interpretations when looking for a field knife. It's not as simple as choosing a survival knife that you think will meet all the outdoor criteria you might have.

Knives should be viewed as a complete system and not as a one size fits all remedy.

All of the knives we have described here will do their job very well as a field knife and for everyday wood carving purposes.

Zippo lighter and windproof matches

Matches of very generous dimensions and capable of releasing monstrous heat. They are encased in a bulletproof watertight container with a nice heavy-duty o-ring. Due to the truly unheard-of size of the matches, the box clearly contains a maximum of 12. This is certainly not a defect since if used well, a match of these corresponds to a lit fire. Necessary in your emergency kit. Why a Zippo and not a classic lighter? Because if you need it to light a fire, especially if the environment is humid and the wood wet, you will have to spend a long time with the flame lit under the kindling so that it can light up and with a normal lighter you would risk burning yourself after a while because the wheel would become hot. With a Zippo instead once you have created the flame, you can stay as long as you want. Moreover, it is rechargeable, and you can also think of bringing a small supply of gas with you.

Water bottle with mess tin

The water bottle with integrated mess tin is convenient for drinking and cooking, saving a lot of space and additional weight compared to those who carry an entire mess tin with various pots and separate water bottles.

✓ The best on the market: Keith Trekking Titanium Bottle

✓ Value for money: Latinaric Stainless Steel

Keith Trekking Titanium bottle

Titanium water bottles are the best ever even if unfortunately, very expensive. Titanium is an element that makes them very light, highly resistant, non-toxic to humans and anti-corrosive. They cost a lot, but they have to be taken into account if we want a definitive bottle that will accompany us throughout our life during our adventures.

Latinaric Water Bottle in Stainless Steel

It is the best stainless-steel bottle you can find around. It comes with a handy case that allows you to attach it to your belt and always have it ready for use.

Paracord

Paracord, as the name also suggests, is the rope that is used to make the parachute, consequently it is an extremely resistant rope, tested to resist tearing and very strong stresses. In essence it is a set of thin nylon strings intertwined with a sheath that encloses them all.

The excellent quality paracord is the one with code 550 and can be recognized because inside it is composed of 7 filaments composed in turn of 3 other nylon filaments. It is indispensable in our equipment for infinite uses including the creation of a shelter with the Tarp.

✓ The Best: Ganzoo Paracord 550 98,4 feet

✓ Value for money: Dilve Paracord 550 328 feet

Ganzoo Paracord 550 98,4 ft

After having tested many of them we can confirm for you that the most resistant of all and therefore the one of the best workmanships remains the Ganzoo.

Dilwe Paracord 550 328 ft

Dilwe Paracord wins the prize for value for money. We know that Paracord is a very resistant and expensive rope which unfortunately is frequently used by adventurers looking for cheaper and more sustainable solutions. Dilwe's Paracord 550 addresses this needs.

Head Torch

- ✓ The most popular: Eecoo (300 Lumens)
- ✓ The most powerful: Eletorot (2000 Lumens)

Ecoo 300 Lumens

An excellent headlamp with 300 Lumens of power and 6 different lighting modes including red. Excellent purchase.

Olight H2R Nova 2300 Lumens

The front torch of the Olight H2R Nova is one of the best around and with a power of 2300 lumens with 5 different lighting modes, it is capable of illuminating the night so much that it almost seems like day. The torch is also removable for handheld use. The Olight house has been at the top in the field of torches for years.

Waterproof poncho

Our pick: Miltech

Miltec Waterproof Poncho

Miltec is a great brand, and this Poncho is among the best ever. The Miltec Poncho is lightweight, rugged and 100% waterproof making it the best choice for your wilderness adventures.

Sleeping bag

- ✓ For fall/winter/spring or temperatures from 0 to 15: Ferrino Yukon Pro
- ✓ For summer: Explorer

Ferrino Yukon Pro

Ferrino has been synonymous with quality for years and this sleeping bag is one of the best solutions on the market for adventures in autumn, winter and spring or in any case for temperatures ranging from -3 degrees to 15.

Explorer

For spring/summer instead opt for the Explorer Sleeping Bag. It has a mummy structure that allows you to shelter if it gets colder than expected and is very compact once it is closed.

Tarp or Tent

For those who want to face more extreme adventures in close contact with nature, we recommend the use of the Tarp. The Tarp is a tarp with many hooks to be used with different combinations depending on the type of shelter we want to create.

As for the tents instead, we will only show you the lightest and single-seater ones.

Pros and Cons of Tarp:
- ✓ Pros: Versatile and lightweight
- ✓ Cons: need for more experience and knot knowledge

Pros and Cons of the Tent:
- ✓ Pros: easy to use and is more protected from insects and atmospheric agents
- ✓ Cons: Much heavier and bulkier

Single-person tents

- ✓ The best: Aqua Quest Hooped
- ✓ Excellent value for money: Miltec

Aqua Quest Hooped Ultralight One-man Tent

Aqua Quest is a very famous and high-quality brand that has always been. This ultralight single-person tent is no exception and is perfect for those who prefer to have more shelter without carrying excessive weight in their backpack with a very small footprint.

Miltec Single Person Tent

Here too Miltec has created an excellent single-person tent at an affordable price and available in different colours. It has convinced us and many other Bushcrafters who have chosen it for their adventures in nature.

Tarp Bushcraft

Now let's talk about the solution most chosen by adventurers who love light equipment and more direct contact with the surrounding nature.
- ✓ The most versatile: DD Hammock 3×3
- ✓ Lightest: Sea to Summit Escapist 3×3
- ✓ The most robust and waterproof: Aqua Quest Defender
- ✓ DD Hammock 3×3

Check availability on Amazon.

This light Tarp is one of the most used in the world, as it is quite robust and very versatile thanks to 19 attachment points.

Sea to Summit Escapist

One of the lightest Tarps on the market used especially for those who do climbing or in general for those who want to minimize the weight of the backpack.

Aqua Quest Defender

The Tarp Aqua Quest Defender is undoubtedly one of the best Tarps around due to its robustness and total impermeability. Based on these two characteristics, it's up to you to choose whether to carry about 1.1. Lbs or 2 more in your backpack but have an almost "immortal" and totally waterproof towel, or to focus on lighter but less robust and less waterproof products.

For example, if you are an expert adventurer and often go to snowy areas, the Tarp Aqua Quest Defender is mandatory in your equipment.

Bushcraft clothing, shirts and trousers

Clothing is connected to the climate of the place you choose to visit. There are no specific rules in this sector, but the important thing is to opt for clothing that is sturdy, comfortable and that can best protect every part of the body. If you choose a cold place, layered clothing is recommended, in order to regulate body temperature and not disperse heat.

Here is a small list for reference:
- Undergarments: Seamless and elastic knickers and undershirts
- Thermal trousers and shirts: insulate from the cold and prevent phenomena such as perspiration.
- Sweaters, sweatshirts, trousers, fleeces, jackets: they form an additional thermal barrier.
- Jackets, over trousers, capes: they protect from atmospheric agents such as wind and rain.
- Gloves, double or thick socks, hats, visors, earmuffs, neck warmers: they offer the ultimate level of protection, going to repair the extremities of the body which are more vulnerable to the cold.
- High boots: protect from cold and foreign bodies.

In summer and in hot places it is necessary to wear clothing that can protect you from the sun and insects, and footwear that protects the foot.

Advanced toolmaking (woodworking, metalworking, etc.)

After listing a whole host of useful tools for the basics of bushcrafting, let's take a look at the slightly more advanced ones.

Tools Make fires in the woods

Anyone who wants to try their hand at bushcraft and survivalism must know the importance of fire Warmth, protection, food and water in a remote situation, fire can provide us with everything we need to survive, it can keep us warm, it can create the necessary to purify water, and it keeps unwanted guests away.

Turn it on with minimal effort.

Lighting a fire in a wild context is not a feat, so having the best equipment to achieve the goal will allow you to save important energies.

There isn't just one Bushcraft fire, but the particularity of the bushcraft fire, compared to the classic survivalist campfire, is that it is a multifunctional fire designed to last.

Ignite with Heliko-Tex Scout fire starter kit stack fire.

We can begin from the easiest to employ. The Helikon-tex fire is starter kit, in which a small fire starter can be found, two fuel cubes and a cotton ball. Obviously, the cotton ball was useful as a trigger, once the cotton was inflamed we transmitted the fire to the flammable cube, after which starting our small pile fire was easy, in conditions we had already set the different layers of fuel, with a consistent bed composed of flakes of dry wood.

The stack the fire

Another kind of practice for lighting a fire is with the gable positioning, this system is also designed to allow easy ignition of the hearth and continuity in combustion without the need for a continuous power supply. The procedure is very simple, first of all the ground is prepared, cleaning and possibly creating a barrier with stones. Then a base is made with small wood, dry wood bark and fuel for starting, after which a first level of small sticks, then you go up with a level of larger sticks and so on until the desired size is formed, once the trigger has started it must be inserted inside the hut and the job is done

Fire Dakota Hole

The Dakota Hole fire is a small campfire, designed to minimize the visibility of the flame, the secret consists in digging two holes in the earth, a main one which will act as a brazier and a secondary one, much smaller which will serve as an air intake. The two holes must be joined by a tunnel for the passage of air, in this way it will be possible to create a comfortable fire for cooking which will offer a discreet source of heat, with a very low visual impact.

Swedish torch

Perfect for cooking, the Swedish torch is the favorite solution of "Swedish" lumberjacks made with an ax or more easily with a chainsaw, it allows you to create a flame inside a trunk, making it easy to position cookware for cooking or boiling.

Woodworking tools

Top 10 best bushcraft knives for woodworking

Woodwork and bushcraft go hand in hand. But not every bushcraft knife can be used for woodworking. But which knife to choose? To make your choice simpler we have made a full list of top 10 bushcraft and woodworking knives.

1. Helle Utvaer 600 outdoor knife

The Helle Utvaer 600 is a versatile bushcraft knife. Thanks to this knife you will be able to work the wood in a simple manner and with the pointed tip you will work with precision. The wood finish is smooth and well-rounded for a comfortable grip. The Helle Utvaer comes with a gorgeous Scandinavian-style leather sheath.

2. Mora Garberg bushcraft knife, multiassembly.

One the most famous knife, the Mora Garberg could be thought as a versatile bushcraft knife. The blade is thinner towards the tip, perfect for more detailed work. The edge start is thicker for more demanding cutting tasks, such as woodworking. Vegetables are not compatible with this knife.

3. Hultafors OK4 Outdoor Knife 4 380270 carbon, fixed knife

The Hultafors Ok4 Outdoor Knife is a famous fixed bushcraft knife. The black layer protects the carbon steel blade from corrosion. It is created to make to utilize the flintlock a breeze. The side of the blade is enhanced with a 5cm long ruler.

Mora Eldris Black 12647 neck knife with sheath

The Mora Eldris is a fixed neck knife. You can wear it around your neck. The perfect partner for little considerate tasks around the field, like food prep and woodwork. The blade is thick just around the edge for more demanding tasks like notching wood. Towards the tip the blade is thinner for more precise tasks.

4. Fällkniven A1 Pro outdoor knife, A1PRO10

The Fällkniven A1 Pro is a high-quality outdoor knife featuring a full-tang handle. This knife is considered one of the sturdier knives on this list. When it comes to steel, Fällkniven opted for CoS steel, which has been known for years.

5. Real Steel Bushcraft III Convex Ebony Mosaic 3726E Knivesandtools Exclusive bushcraft knife

It is a kind all-rounder bushcraft knife. The convex edge is bond and makes the cuts in a perfect way. Considering the price, it could represents an amazing option. The blade is composed of D2 steel: a robust steel that retains its sharpness. In addition, it is resistant to breakage and is also simply to sharpen. You have to pay attention to acids, salt and humidity: D2 is not completely stainless. We, however, feel that this does not outweigh the benefits of this tough steel grade.

6. Helle JS 200676 Limited Edition 2022, bushcraft knife, design by Jan Steffen Helle.

The Helle JS 200676 is a bushcraft knife, designed by Jan Steffen Helle. This is the nephew of Sigmund Helle, one of the founders of the brand. The steel employed for its building is Helle's signature proprietary steel type: a core of hard stainless steel, surrounded by layers of 18/8 stainless steel. The knife is extremely sharp and is also easy to sharpen, perfect for woodworking.

7. Roselli Carpenter Knife R110 leather sheath

It is a well-made fixed knife, made in the north Europe. Finland for being more precise. Unique to Roselli is UHC: Ultra High Carbon steel. At Roselli they have specifically distribute this kind of carbon steel, and also its unique heat treatment setting for great performance. Without it becoming brittle!

8. Karesuando Vuonjal 3633 outdoor knife

The Karesuando Vuonjal is a typical Scandinavian outdoor knife. The handle is made of birch wood. Vuonjal it is also one of the most elegant knives on this list thanks to a stunning brass bolster embellishing.

Camp crafts (baskets, mats, containers, etc.)

Let's see briefly instead what the tools for camp crafts are:

Baskets

Baskets, or woven baskets, are an important part of the bushcraft and craft traditions of many cultures. Baskets can be used for a variety of purposes, such as picking berries, storing food, transporting items, or building shelters.

For giving life to a bushcraft-style basket, selecting the right raw materials is required. Typically, plant fibers are used, such as tree bark, palm leaves, tree roots or branches. When all the raw materials have been gathered, they should be set and handled to make them adaptable for employ.

The process of creating the basket begins with the collection and preparation of plant fibers. These are cleaned, bleached and dried in the sun. Afterwards, they are intertwined to create the shape of the basket. There are several weaving techniques that can be used to create baskets of different shapes and sizes.

Once the basket is complete, it can be customized by adding decorations or handles to make it easier to carry. The baskets can also be treated with oil or wax to make them more resistant to water and bad weather.

Creating a bushcraft-style basketball takes skill, patience, and knowledge of weaving techniques. However, the end result is a practical, durable and good-looking object that can be used for many different purposes. Additionally, creating a woven basket can be a rewarding experience and a way to connect with nature and the craft traditions of the past.

Mats

Mats are important elements in bushcraft and can be used for multiple purposes, such as protection from cold and damp, as a support for rest, as a work surface for food preparation, as a base for starting a fire and more. There are several kinds of mats, each with its own features and pros. One of the most employed materials for making mats is tree bark, like birch or pine bark. The bark is stripped from the tree and processed to create a smooth, level surface that can be used as a base for sleeping or working. Another common material for making mats is dry grass or hay. These materials can be woven together to create a thick, fluffy rug that offers protection from cold and wet conditions.

Plant leaves can also be useful to create mats. For example, fern leaves can be woven together to create a thick, durable surface that can be used as a support for rest or as a base for making a fire.

Finally, animal skins can be used to make mats, especially those of animals such as deer or bison. These mats are thick and soft, offer optimal protection from cold and wet conditions and can be used as a sleeping base or work surface.

Creating mats requires knowledge and skill in selecting and working with materials, but the end result is a practical and useful item that can be used in many bushcraft situations.

Containers

Bushcraft containers are essential tools for survival in the wilderness. They allow you to store, carry, and transport food, water, fire-making materials, and other necessary items. Here are some common types of bushcraft containers:

- ✓ Water bottles: A durable, leak-proof water bottle is a must-have in any bushcraft kit. Look for bottles made of stainless steel or other rugged materials that can withstand rough handling and outdoor conditions.
- ✓ Cookware: A lightweight and durable cookware set is essential for cooking and preparing meals in the wild. Look for pots and pans made of titanium, stainless steel, or other heat-resistant materials that can withstand high temperatures.
- ✓ Storage containers: For storing food, spices, and other small items, consider using a set of stackable plastic containers with snap-on lids. They can be considerate as waterproof, lightweight, and simple to pack.
- ✓ Dry bags: A dry bag is an essential tool for keeping your gear dry when crossing rivers or during heavy rain. Look for a bag made of durable, waterproof material with a roll-top closure that seals out water.
- ✓ Backpacks: this is a vital bushcraft container that can contain all your gear and supplies. The only thing you should do for a perfect bushcraft backpack is opting for a multiple compartments and pockets one. This could be helpful for organization and simple access.

How to maintain and care for your tools

Maintaining bushcraft tools is truly essential to make you quite sure they are always ready to employ and will last. Below there are some tips to maintain them in good condition for long time:

- ✓ Cleaning: After any employ, you should clean tools thoroughly with mild soap and water, making sure to take off any dirt or residue. After having done this, you should dry the tools well with the aim of a dry cloth.
- ✓ Oil: To prevent rust and keep tools sharp, apply a thin coat of preservative oil to the blade, hatchet, or other metal tool.
- ✓ Storage: store the tools in a dry and dust-free place, preferably in a specific case or container.

- ✓ Sharpening: Keep tools sharpened regularly to ensure they cut efficiently. Use a sharpening stone or sharpening file, following the manufacturer's instructions.
- ✓ Periodic Inspection: Regularly check tools for damage or wear and repair or replace if necessary.

By following these tips, you will be able to keep your bushcraft tools in good condition and ready to use at all times.

Chapter 2: First Aid and Medical Emergencies

This chapter will cover the importance of first aid in the wilderness, basic first aid skills, common medical emergencies, and how to create a first aid kit. It will also be focused on how to prepare for medical emergencies when you will find yourself in the wilderness.

The importance of first aid in the wilderness

First aid is the set of actions that make it possible to help, in emergency situations, one or more people in difficulty, victims of physical or psychological trauma or sudden illness, while awaiting the arrival of qualified rescuers.

First aid also means assistance that is given in temporary structures in the presence of critical situations, while waiting to transport the patient to more adequately equipped health centers.

The objectives of first aid are to analyze the emergency situation to understand if it is necessary to alert advanced rescue services, and subsequently offer the assistance requested, making sure not to cause further damage to the individual.

In this case, attending the bushcraft environment, from simple excursions to rock routes, inevitably involves risks that can lead to accidents. We can have hikers with minor injuries or with serious, sometimes fatal, injuries.

As mentioned on other occasions, if we go into the woods aware of the risks and prepared from all points of view, these accidents can be avoided. But in any case, it is good to know how bushcraft first aid works.

Key word: prevention is better than cure

As you will have understood by now, in general but even more in the woods, the basic rule "prevention is better than cure" is more current than ever. Many accidents that we hear on TV or read in the newspaper can very well be avoided: very often, in fact, a whole set of factors that considerably increase the risk of injury are underestimated. Old and unsafe equipment, unfavorable weather conditions, incorrect diet, poor training and physical preparation, lack of sleep, superficiality, are all causes that can easily lead to an accident.

The accident can be minor but sometimes it can be a serious accident and unfortunately in some circumstances even fatal. So, we reiterate the concept that to go to the mountains you need to plan the excursion well at home, have the right preparation and be informed and prepared about everything, without leaving anything out. In this way we go to work on the subjective dangers (i.e. that depend on us) leaving a minimum percentage of accident probability to chance.

For example, one thing to always keep in your backpack is the first aid kit with plasters and basic medicines (disinfectant, gauze, etc.) which can be very useful if necessary. Let's see what the behaviors are to follow in the event of an accident and what are the basic maneuvers to perform before help arrives. You need to pay close attention because first aid (i.e., all the methods and procedures that are adopted before the intervention of the emergency services) is not mandatory but in some cases, it could save the life of the injured person or avoid worse damage before the intervention of the rescuers. This is why we speak of the crime of omission. Obviously, in certain circumstances knowing and being able to apply certain first aid maneuvers is essential to save the life of the injured person.

First aid: why is it so important?

Because first aid maneuvers are decisive for subsequent evolution and can make the difference between life and death. In certain situations, the interventions and maneuvers carried out in the very short term with respect to a possible accident play a decisive role in the subsequent evolution of the situation from the point of view of health and physical integrity.

In particular, some first aid maneuvers, if carried out adequately and knowing the correct methods, can be decisive with respect to the patient's chances of survival. In other cases, where survival is not at stake, they can still be decisive in avoiding even serious complications.

I call 911 anyway: Ok1 Only that this approach could be a death sentence.

A very important reminder: calling 911 is of the utmost importance. The assistance of emergency medical personnel is essential. But that's not always possible. And in any case, whoever answers is not on the spot.

To understand why this is an inappropriate statement, just think of two aspects: How much time do we have to save the life of a person in cardiac arrest? Few minutes. What are the chances that in this period it will be possible to get personnel from the emergency health service (911) to arrive on site after having alerted the emergency services? As fast and efficient as the service is, a lot, but very few. The chance of intervening immediately and in a proper manner can therefore make the difference between life and death.

Basic first aid skills

Let's see what the basic first aid and skills are.

The accident and the examination of the injured

If you are in the woods with a friend or a group of people and an accident happens, the absolutely thing to do is not to panic and act rationally and quickly. Once you have reached your partner (safely without putting your life at risk) you put him in a safe position, and you go on to evaluate the traumatized person. In this way we will give more precise indications to the rescue machine.

The most frequent forms of accidents in the mountains or in the woods are due to falls along the path and traumas caused by stone discharges. If we are able and have knowledge of first aid, we proceed otherwise once we understand the conditions of the partner, we must immediately call the emergency services and wait for help to arrive.

We want you to remind that by law we are not obliged to perform resuscitation maneuvers (we could do worse), but we are obliged to call 911. There are three initial maneuvers to do:

- ✓ Check the state of consciousness.
- ✓ Check respiratory function.
- ✓ Check heart function.

State of consciousness

In this first phase (to be done within 2-3 minutes) we evaluate whether the patient is awake and understand things, then we proceed to evaluate the state of the chest and abdomen, and then we proceed to verify the mobility and sensitivity of the limbs to evaluate possible fractures, contusions, dislocations, hemorrhages, etc. or at worst trauma to the spinal cord.

Respiratory function

In this second phase, it is checked whether the injured person is breathing spontaneously (watching if the chest rises and falls and if air comes out of the mouth) and if so, it is checked that vomit, blood, mud is blocking the airways. It is important, in this phase, to also observe the color of the skin: bluish gray is synonymous with poor oxygenation and therefore respiratory deficiencies, a pale color is synonymous with hemorrhage or a state of shock.

Heart function

In this phase the heartbeat is checked by placing the ear on the injured person's chest and examining the peripheral points to check the correct flow of blood: wrists, neck and femur.

What are the first aid maneuvers.

First aid maneuvers become fundamental once we have examined the injured person and we have noticed some anomaly. Once the injured person has been examined, we must immediately alert the rescue operations machine, but in certain cases, knowing how to perform particular maneuvers can be of great help and save lives. To perform these maneuvers, however, you need to be able to do them otherwise once the call to the rescue has been made, we don't have to do anything except do what the operator tells us to do on the telephone.

The basic maneuver, very important, and that each of us should know how to do is cardiopulmonary resuscitation (CPR) and consists in performing artificial respiration and cardiac massage. From cardiac arrest we have about 3 minutes before the brain suffers permanent damage, so it is essential to intervene immediately, as long as we wait for the Alpine Rescue. As fast as they are, 10-15 minutes can easily pass between call and intervention; this is why it is important to know how to examine the injured person and give precise indications to the operator on the other side of the telephone.

The signals that state the need for a R.C.P. are:
- ✓ Cardiac arrest
- ✓ Respiratory arrest
- ✓ Loss of consciousness
- ✓ Fixed mydriasis (abnormally dilated pupils)
- ✓ Bluish-gray skin tone.

Fractures and bleeding: how to recognize them and what to do

The two most frequent cases that could occur in the event of an accident are fractures and bleeding. Even in these cases it is important to recognize them and know what to do to alleviate the pain and damage caused by the wounds.

Fractures

The fracture is the breaking of a bone, and this is evident when there is:
- ✓ Ache
- ✓ Movement difficulties
- ✓ Swelling and bleeding
- ✓ Deformations due to displacement of the bone
- ✓ Mobility abnormality
- ✓ More or less large wounds with the protrusion of the broken bone (open fracture).

The important thing to do is to immobilize the affected limb with whatever is available (bands, string, pieces of wood, etc.) to immobilize the bone so that it cannot move.

Splinting

The thorns and small splinters can be very annoying, and result in various complications. Think of the thorns of a fruit, a hedgehog, a cactus or even a plant. As for splinters, they range from an object that breaks in our hands, to wood residue. The very first thing to do, both in the case of a thorn and a splinter, is to wash the affected part well with clean, fresh water, then dry and disinfect the area to avoid the onset of an infection. Once this is done, what to do to remove a splinter from the finger in depth or a thorn without a needle (perhaps without pain)? Fortunately, we have several useful ways to find immediate relief and avoid potential risks to our health. To each thorn or chip its method. The very small spines are virtually impossible to remove with bare hands. It is already a lot if we can clearly distinguish its presence on the skin. In cases like this, the only possible solution is to resort to eyebrow tweezers, previously sanitized and dried. But proceed with great delicacy, as the plug could break at the climax. To those who wonder if water and salt are effective for removing thorns in this specific case, we answer that they can help in some way. Mostly to disinfect the skin.

How to remove a splinter of glass

If the glass shard has an external part that protrudes from the skin, the ideal solution is to grab it with washed and disinfected make-up tweezers. However, it is an operation that must be carried out very delicately to prevent it from breaking inside. If this should happen, however, nothing is lost: whether it is a thorn or a splinter broken inside the skin, you can use a needle disinfected with alcohol or hydrogen peroxide and make room, with its tip, to create a way out. In any case, when it comes to small fragments, the body can also reject the foreign body autonomously after a few days through an inflammatory phenomenon.

How to remove a wood splinter

If you wonder how to remove a splinter of wood, know that you can proceed with one of the methods already seen above. Or you can be patient and wait for the skin, regenerating itself thanks to its natural renewal, to expel it by itself. Another tool that we have available, is to apply an ichthyol ointment on the area for splinters which, thanks to its astringent power, facilitates this operation, but only if these are superficial. Thus, the splinters come out by themselves, without forcing or particular interventions. Finally, you can try to remove a splinter with oil: to do this, just apply it using a cotton ball and leave it on for a few minutes. This is a manner to make the skin soften and make the extraction much simpler.

Bleeding and wounds

Bleeding occurs when there is blood loss and can be of two types: venous and arterial.
A venous hemorrhage is identified when blood comes out slowly but steadily in a deep red color. It may be useful to compress the wound with bandages and gauze fixed with a bandage, or with simple plasters after disinfecting the wound. If the wound affects a limb, it could be useful to keep it raised with respect to the body.
Arterial hemorrhages, on the other hand, are the most dangerous ones because they affect the arteries. In this case the blood comes out as a spray, synchronous with the heartbeat, of a bright red color. The thing to do is apply a finger by pressing directly on the lesion or at most put a tourniquet upstream of the wound but no more than an hour's time. The tourniquet (or belts, ties or similar) must not be used in an attempt to stop the bleeding upstream of the wound and must be used only in cases of absolute necessity and with extreme caution: for example, before an amputation or a crush syndrome.

Waiting for help

The best position to adopt is the supine position with the legs high compared to the body to allow blood to flow better to the vital organs. If the injured person is in a state of unconsciousness, the safety position must be adopted. Another thing to do while we wait for help is to cover our companion with a thermal sheet so that he does not disperse too much heat. You should never give him anything to drink because he could choke, but if he is conscious you can give him something to eat in case he is hungry. It is also vital to verify at regular intervals and monitor the patient's condition, and at the same time waiting for the right help.

Common medical emergencies

Let's see what common medical emergencies in bushcraft could be.

Hypothermia

Hypothermia is normally due by prolonged exposure to cold and happens once the human body drops below 95°F. At the first feeling of cold, you should therefore wear warmer clothing. Especially on long bushcraft trips in the environment, warm and windproof clothing is essential even if the sun is shining during the ascent. Sudden bad weather shadows or wind can greatly accentuate the danger. Symptoms of hypothermia are:

- ✓ Shivering, pale and cold
- ✓ Apathy and disorientation
- ✓ Slow and shallow breathing
- ✓ Slow and weak pulse

in case of exposure to cold and damage of the peripheral parts of the body (fingers and toes, nose and ears), it is frostbite.

Treatment of hypothermia

Here you are the practices to do:
- ✓ The hypothermia subject should be warmed up slowly. You can do it by covering the victim with blankets and a cap.
- ✓ Whenever possible provide a hot drink and/or high energy food (like chocolate) to the person.
- ✓ Call 911 for help.
- ✓ Monitor the victim's vital signs, respiration, temperature and state of consciousness, until the ambulance arrives.

In all cases, protect the person from the cold.
- ✓ Move it to a sheltered and heated environment.
- ✓ Remove cold clothing, especially if wet, only if it is possible to protect against the cold and cover the person with dry clothing, blankets or towels.

- ✓ Warm the injured person with hot water bags in the armpits or groin.
- ✓ Warning: never put hot water bottles in direct contact with the skin.

Dehydration

When you practice bushcraft in the summer and walk big there is an invisible enemy to always keep under control: dehydration! With the high temperatures and the effort of walking, our body loses a lot of fluids and thirst can come too late.

In this period of the year walking in nature is a real delight, the beautiful days and the late setting sun are ideal conditions for enjoying trekking, especially in the woods and in the high mountains.

These climatic conditions, even in the mountains where it is cooler, are not always a good thing, in fact bushcraft is an intense and prolonged effort activity, which involves a lot of sweating.

During a day's walk, through sweating and accelerated respiratory rate, you can lose up to 2 liters of fluids per hour.

This is the motivation about the fact to never to forget to replace liquids and mineral salts.

In the body, water performs essential functions, keeps the body temperature constant and allows the body to function properly.

For this reason, when its percentage begins to drop, the body begins to absorb liquids from the blood, making it denser, a circumstance that affects the oxygenation of organs and muscles.

The most common symptoms

The most common symptom is thirst, even if this is not always perceived immediately and, above all, it is not proportional to the level of dehydration.

Symptoms such as dry mouth, muscle cramps, a widespread sense of tiredness and dryness of the mucous membranes are indicators of an important state of dehydration, this is the time to stop and drink water or, even better, saline supplements.

Often, however, these symptoms are considered almost "normal" and some continue to walk without paying due attention.

In the next stage, our body signals the need for liquids through unequivocal manifestations, such as dizziness, headaches and constipation.

These symptoms cannot be ignored, the level of dehydration is quite advanced, when these signs arise it is advisable to take a break, to rest and drink mineral salt supplements.

Up to this point we have talked about situations in which it is sufficient to drink some water or, at the most, allow yourself a refreshment break and a salt supplement.

These behaviors are enough to regain strength and continue walking.

In some cases, however, the situation may require medical intervention, there are symptoms that are the sign of a very serious state of dehydration.

The danger level is reached when the person begins to be in a state of confusion, to be irritable and disoriented, the mouth becomes very dry, the eyes sunken, the skin wrinkled, and the heart rate accelerates.

This is the time to stop and interrupt the bushcraft activities, if these signs appear, it is absolutely not recommended to continue the journey and it is advisable to request the intervention of medical personnel.

Water and supplements always in the backpack

These are the reasons why every hiker's backpack should never lack water and saline supplements.

This is because in addition to liquids, mineral salts are also lost through sweating.

The best saline supplements on the market have a combination of salts and antioxidants specifically designed to counteract dispersion during intense physical activity, such as bushcraft, which often lasts for several hours and, especially in summer, causes a significant loss of fluids.

In conclusion we can say that during a bushcraft excursion it is better to drink at regular intervals, without waiting for the stimulus of thirst to appear.

How to create a first aid kit

Let's see how to create a first aid kit for our bushcraft activities. Among the thousand things that must be in the bushcraft backpack, there is one that is indispensable: the first aid kit. What characterizes it is that it contains everything needed to deal with a health emergency in a small space.

What should a survival first aid kit contain?

When deciding which first aid kit is right for you, think about the places you usually frequent. Generally, plasters of various sizes, gauze and pain relievers will already be in your starter kit. However, if you plan to venture to places known to be food-hazardous, make sure your kit includes anti-nausea medications. If you go camping, a burn ointment, antihistamine ointment, and eye drops may help. If you go backpacking, you will need to have a cream with you to protect yourself from blisters.

In any case, the emergency kit must contain everything needed for camping or any outdoor activity.

It must also be easy to place in the car, in your bag or to keep at home so that you always have some basic first aid accessories. It must also have everything needed for basic injuries, such as, for example: minor cuts, sprains, burns, minor injuries.

In your kit there must be:
- Sterile pads
- Scissors
- Adhesive plasters
- Alcohol-free wipes
- Small and large safety pins
- Rolls of tape
- 2 pairs of medium gloves
- 1 conforming bandage
- 1 triangular bandage.
- Butterfly closures
- Cpr mask
- Gauze
- Tweezers
- Medical scissors
- Remove splinters.

In addition to these items, your first aid backpack (or bag) also includes some extra pockets inside to add other essentials such as paracetamol, allergy medications and anything else you want to have on hand.

How to prepare for medical emergencies in the wilderness

In emergencies wilderness situations, you may be temporarily lonely. What happens, for example, when floods, landslides or rock falls make roads impassable? In these cases, self-protection and personal responsibility play an important role. Those who take the right precautions for themselves and their fellow human beings and who have the necessary knowledge can help themselves and overcome the critical phase more calmly until help arrives or the emergency situation ends.

Personal emergency supplies

Most of the dangers can be avoided or the harmful effects can be kept within limits by acting sensibly. Self-protection also includes being well prepared on your bushcraft excursions for disasters. A supply of drinks, food and first aid kit should not be missing.

Read a first aid manual carefully

Indeed, a course or light should be taken, and a comprehensive manipulative has the sole purpose of enabling the average person to manage injuries, infections, wounds and chronic and acute illnesses in situations where modern medical facilities are not available due to a disaster or simply because immersed in wild nature and unable to go to the nearest hospital or waiting to buy time waiting for help. Both a course and a manual explain how to be prepared for various emergencies, illustrating the main skills necessary for survival; what to bring along for medical emergencies and how to manage first aid to save a life; how to survive with few materials, showing you how to make bandages and splints in nature and how to use plants to extract dressings. From cuts to burns, fractures to injuries, these manuals or courses are all you need to be ready for all your outdoor adventures and face any emergency.

PART 6: WILDERNESS SURVIVALIST MINDSET

Chapter 1: Survival Psychology and Mindset

The importance of a positive mindset in survival situations

Maintaining a positive mindset in survival situations is extremely important. When in an emergency or survival situation, it can be easy to fall into despair, anxiety, and fear. However, maintaining a positive mindset can mean the difference between life and death.

A positive mindset helps you stay calm and focused on stressful situations. When you're worried or scared, it's easy to get confused and lose sight of your main goals. However, if you keep a positive mindset and focus on finding solutions, you can stay calm and work towards finding a way out of the bind.

Additionally, a positive mindset can help maintain optimism and hope in difficult situations. When one feels overwhelmed by circumstances, it can be easy to lose hope and believe there is no way to survive. However, maintaining a positive mindset can help maintain hope and a belief that a solution can be found.

Finally, a positive mindset can help improve mental and physical health in survival situations. When experiencing an emergency or survival situation, it's easy to feel overwhelmed, stressed, and depressed. However, maintaining a positive mental attitude can help reduce stress and improve mood, which can in turn improve physical and mental health.

How to stay calm and focused in stressful situations

In difficult situations it is hard to keep calm, especially if you are experiencing a period of severe stress. But it's not impossible.

Especially when you're under stress, faced with difficult situations it seems impossible not to lose control.

Stress, if you know how to manage it and keep it at a low level, is not harmful but rather helps you train your ability to adapt in difficult situations such as survival, and to face problems to achieve your goals.

Learning how to stay calm is very important, and sometimes essential, to avoid panicking and losing control, thus allowing yourself to be overwhelmed by negative emotions associated with situations of intense physical or emotional stress.

Knowing how to keep calm in the face of critical events and situations is undoubtedly a virtue of a few. The most common reactions, in fact, are the biological ones of flight, fight or paralysis, which are accompanied by emotions such as:

- Fear
- Anger
- Impotence

Obviously, experiencing feelings of fear, anger or a sense of helplessness is completely normal and human in extreme situations. The problem arises when these reactions lead to mental and physical paralysis in situations where it is necessary to react.

Since security is a vital need and calmness is that mental resource that helps you stay in the so-called safety zone in the face of real danger or a threat of danger, it is very important to learn how to regulate your emotional response to be able to face extreme situations and the associated threat and dangers, calmly and steadfastly.

But how to keep calm in stressful situations and difficult situations involving survival in the wild?

The first thing to do is stop and breathe deeply. When you feel yourself losing self-control, try to be silent for 20 seconds. By doing this, you will be able to recognize the situation earlier that will cause you to lose calm and concentration, and you will be able to deal with it better.

The second thing you absolutely must do is make the situation as safe as possible. Seek shelter from bad weather or obvious dangers. This can help reduce your anxiety and make you feel more confident.

Another way to always stay clear-headed and focused is to make a plan. Try to prioritize and make an action plan.

Surely a solution to not lose your temper and find yourself in dangerous situations is to maintain self-confidence. Focus on your abilities and resources and try to maintain your self-confidence.

A very effective tip to not lose calm and lucidity is to practice mindfulness. The practice of mindfulness can help you avoid dangerous situations, as it allows you to stay present and attentive to your actions and your surroundings. For example, to be aware, it is good that he recognizes danger signs. Be alert for warning signs in your surroundings, such as weather conditions, aggressive people or animals, dangerous areas, and so on. Being aware of these signs can help you make informed decisions and avoid dangerous situations. Also, mindfulness will keep you from doing dangerous or risky things. For example, don't climb unstable objects or walk in areas known to have dangerous animals.

Another very effective way to deal with dangerous situations and stay focused is visualization. Visualization is a great technique for preparing to face dangerous situations. Imagine the dangerous situation in your mind. Try to imagine all the details, such as your surroundings, the people involved, the weather conditions. Imagine yourself dealing with the situation safely and effectively. Visualize yourself making informed decisions, using your skills and resources, and facing danger with confidence. Identify the specific actions you need to take to address the threatening situation. For example, you may need to seek cover or evacuate the area. Imagine yourself successfully completing the actions you have identified. Visualize the positive outcome, such as your safety and overcoming the dangerous situation. Finally, repeat the visualization several times, in order to fix in your mind, the actions to be taken and the feeling of security that comes from imagining yourself facing the dangerous situation.

Finally, and to put an end to these stressful situations, always remember that the best way to deal with everything is to act. In a dangerous situation, it's important to act quickly and safely to protect yourself and others. Acting in dangerous situations requires calmness, assessment of the situation, protection of oneself and others, contact with the competent authorities and keeping the situation under control.

How to deal with fear and anxiety

Fear can be a natural emotion in bushcraft situations, but it can also be a hindrance to safety and survival. One thing is certain: it is not possible to overcome fear using reason, emotions follow different logics from rational ones.

To defuse automatic reactions before panic explodes, it is necessary to follow these same logics to channel emotional energy in a constructive way.

Fear is a primary emotion, important for our survival, especially if it is linked to real risks. When fear is denied or repressed it can lead to underestimating potential dangers and exposing yourself to major risks. In other cases, if fear is not managed effectively, the dangers may be overestimated, and the fear may escalate into panic.

If you can see her as a friend who comes to your rescue, then she will become a valuable ally and you can use her energy to your advantage. However, this is not always easy because fear is a very powerful emotion and very often it can cause difficulties.

Our mind, by its nature, is programmed to predict and anticipate possible dangers. The function of this automatic mechanism is to protect us and ensure our survival.

Fear, in fact, triggers a physiological reaction in our body which in case of danger prepares us to attack or flee. This adrenaline rush allows us to react quickly to defend ourselves or run away in the face of a threat.

The belief that you can't make it, that you're not good enough, that you don't have enough resources can be paralyzing. The worst effect of this limiting belief is to block any attempt to act on an unpleasant situation, with the risk of passively enduring it. Only if we face fear can we face it and tame it. If we don't do it, denying or repressing it, the risk is that fear takes us in the very direction we would like to avoid. The only solution is to use the emotional charge of fear to channel one's energies towards effective and strategic actions.

Here's how to handle fear in extreme situations:

- Try to always be prepared for any eventuality. Preparation is the key to reducing fear. Acquire survival and bushcraft knowledge and skills and equip yourself with the necessary equipment.
- When you feel fear, try to breathe deeply and slowly. This helps calm the mind and reduce stress.
- Be realistic about the situation. Carefully weigh the danger and try to understand what your options are. Don't let fear overwhelm you but try to think rationally.
- Face fear gradually and with patience. Start with activities that challenge you little by little, and then gradually increase the challenge.
- Team up. Going through bushcraft situations together with other people can help reduce fear. Try to team up with other people and work together to overcome challenges.

How to prepare mentally for survival situations

Mentally preparing for survival situations in the wild can help you deal more confidently with any unforeseen events that may occur during excursions or in emergency situations. Here are some tips on how to prepare yourself mentally:

Be aware of the situation. Search for information about the place you are about to visit. Find out what the most common hazards are, what wildlife might be present, what the typical weather conditions are for the area, etc. Look closely at the terrain to identify potential hazards such as rivers, steep slopes, unstable rocks or other obstacles that could cause problems.

Prepare for emergencies: Carry a survival kit, which includes basic tools like a compass, knife, lighter, and first aid kit.

Follow safety guidelines: Always follow safety guidelines when out in the wild. These include using marked trails, respecting wild animals and using appropriate equipment.

Develop knowledge and skills. Learn the skills needed to survive emergencies in the wild, such as foraging for food, building shelter, fire management, and orienteering.

Mentally Prepare for Inexperience: Accept the fact that emergency situations in nature are unpredictable and unexpected events may occur. Mentally prepare yourself to deal with inexperience and be flexible in your response.

Develop a Survival Mindset: Develop a survival mindset that will help you stay calm and focused on emergency situations. Focus on your short-term goals and finding solutions.

Experience controlled stressful situations: Experience controlled stressful situations, such as camping in inclement weather or navigating difficult situations.

The role of mindfulness and meditation in bushcraft

Mindfulness and meditation can play an important role in bushcrafting, as they help develop mindfulness, inner calm, and the ability to react appropriately in emergency situations.

Mindfulness is easiest to achieve when it is practiced in nature. And at the same time the well-being of nature depends on our awareness.

In bushcrafting, mindfulness can help you stay focused and present when preparing materials, building shelters, starting fires, and other survival activities. Additionally, mindfulness can help manage stress and anxiety during emergency situations.

Mindfulness can help you stay calm and clear-headed during emergency situations, such as when you get lost in an unfamiliar area or need to find food and water. In addition, awareness can help you recognize your body's signals, such as thirst, hunger, fatigue, dehydration or hypothermia, and respond accordingly to avoid incurring health problems.

Mindfulness can be practiced in many ways, such as observing the breath, focusing one's attention on an object or sound, or observing physical sensations. In the practice of bushcraft, awareness can be developed through concentration on the activity that is taking place, observation of the surrounding nature and recognition of one's physical sensations.

Additionally, mindfulness can help develop greater attention to detail, enhancing the ability to recognize plants, animals, and natural resources that can be used for survival.

Meditation is a practice that can be very useful in the context of bushcraft, as it helps to develop greater awareness of oneself and one's surroundings. There are many reasons why we meditate: we relax the mind, we try to make our vital energy flow better, we try to get closer to the present moment.

The approach to nature, thanks to the beauty of the passages, the sounds that permeate the environment and the quality of the air you breathe, helps concentration and gives an extra sprint to achieve a deeper and more lasting state of meditation.

Meditation can help reduce stress and anxiety, increase concentration and the ability to make decisions in emergency situations, as well as improve the ability to learn and adapt to unexpected situations.

Meditation can help you develop greater attention to the present moment. However, it allowing you to observe your thoughts and emotions without being overwhelmed by them. This skill can be very useful in emergency situations, as it helps to maintain calm and clarity in the face of stressful or dangerous situations.

Additionally, meditation can help develop greater empathy and understanding of others, improving the ability to work in teams and collaborate with others in survival situations. Meditation can also help you develop a greater connection with nature, enabling you to appreciate the beauty and complexity of the natural world and to act more responsibly towards your environment.

PART 7: WEATHER AND SURVIVALISM SKILLS

Chapter 1: Weather and Climate

The importance of understanding weather and climate in bushcraft

Understanding the weather and climate is of paramount importance in bushcrafting, as it can mean the difference between a good experience and a dangerous one. Bushcraft is an activity that requires a thorough understanding of the natural environment, including the weather and climate.

The weather can affect many aspects of bushcraft, such as equipment selection, activity planning and safety. For example, if rainy weather is forecast, you need a waterproof tent and a good weather protection system to avoid getting wet and cold. Conversely, if the weather is dry and hot, it's important to bring enough water to avoid dehydration.

The climate is just as important to consider. Some regions may have extremely hot or cold weather, which can affect your choice of equipment and survival techniques. For example, in a region with a hot, dry climate, you need to know ways to get water and keep your body hydrated. Conversely, in a region with a cold climate, it is important to have adequate protection from the cold to avoid hypothermia.

Furthermore, the weather and climate can also affect the safety of the excursion. For example, heavy rains can cause flooding and landslides, while high winds can make walking on steep terrain dangerous. Understanding the weather and climate conditions helps you plan your route and prevent dangerous situations.

Basic meteorology

There is elementary information useful for better interpreting weather maps, knowing how to interpret the sky, being able to predict the weather.

Here are some:

- High pressure. It is the area characterized by a descent of air from top to bottom; from the center of the area, the air moves towards the periphery, sliding towards the low-pressure zone. High pressure is also defined as anticyclone. The high-pressure zones are therefore characterized by clear skies, low temperatures when the sun goes down, and frequent nights with frosts or fog formations.

- Low pressure. The air rises upwards: as the pressure decreases as it rises, the air expands and cools down: thus, the process of condensation of the water vapor, clouds and precipitations are formed. The low-pressure area is called a subtropical cyclone.
- Coriolis effect. It is a deviation of the winds due to the rotation of the earth. The winds at high altitudes are currents with low atmospheric pressure; land winds are high pressure currents. If the Earth did not rotate, the movement of warm air masses over cold air masses would be linear. The rotation of the earth causes the air masses in the northern hemisphere to move from west to east, therefore the perturbations or cyclones come, in the case of Europe, from the Atlantic Ocean and head towards the east. The large displacements of air constitute the atmospheric fronts: whether they are produced by warm air (warm front), or by cold air (cold front), they always bring precipitation, albeit with different consequences and results.
- The clouds. They are composed of particles of water or ice that have condensed around tiny nuclei of aerosols, dust or chemicals. There are different types of clouds, classified according to their shape, height, thickness and color. The main types of clouds are:
  - Cirrus clouds: they are thin, white clouds, which are found at very high altitudes (about 5-10 km) and are mainly composed of ice crystals.
  - Stratiform clouds: they are flat and horizontal clouds, which form at medium-low heights (from 1 to 5 km) and often cover the entire sky. They are made up of water droplets and can produce light rain.
  - Cumulus clouds: they are swollen and voluminous clouds, which form at medium-low heights (from 1 to 5 km) and often have the shape of cumulus clouds or towers. They are composed of water droplets or ice crystals and often produce heavy rain or thunderstorms.
  - Stratocumulus clouds: they are cumulus-shaped clouds, but which develop over a flat horizon like stratiform clouds.
  - Nimbostratus Clouds: These are low, dense clouds that often cover the entire sky and produce heavy rain or snow. They are made up of water droplets or ice crystals.
  - Clouds are important for climate and weather, influencing the amount of solar radiation reaching the earth's surface, the distribution of precipitation and the formation of extreme weather events. Understanding clouds and their behavior is essential for forecasting the weather and managing weather-related risks.
- Lightning. Lightning is caused by two electrical potential differences between the cloud and the underlying ground. Each cloud is charged with a lot of electricity (perhaps due to the friction between the drops of water, moved by the wind and forming the cloud). This electricity discharges to the ground during the thunderstorm. There are two types of lightning: the first consists of an electric discharge from the cloud to the ground; the second from ground to cloud. The latter are much more frequent, as can be seen from the measurements made by the electrical activity control

system, present on the lightning page. These two types are due precisely to the type of electric charge formed.

- The hail. The ascent of warm air up to 10 km of altitude, where temperatures are below zero °C, produces the condensation of humidity. Within an hour of starting the process the rain is heavy. The existing wind allows the hailstones to rise and fall several times in the cloud and to load themselves with more water each time, which will enlarge the grain of ice. Reached a weight beyond the limit allowed by the winds, a hailstorm occurs and the cloud dissolves with light rain.

Reading weather patterns

Knowing how to read and recognize the signals that nature provides is essential to be able to predict, avoid and/or reduce the risks caused by sudden changes in weather conditions. For example, a very frequent and dangerous thing in the mountains is that in a few minutes a beautiful sunny day with mild temperatures turns into an unpleasant situation of bad weather (rain, fog, snow, etc.) with a notable drop in temperature (up to below freezing point). Hence the importance of knowing how to observe and recognize the elements and behavioral patterns of animals and plants, thanks to which it is possible to gain essential minutes to stay safe.

Wind can provide important short- and long-term insights into climate and weather conditions. Here is some information that you can understand based on the wind:

- Observe wind direction: Wind direction can provide information about the air masses present in each area. For example, winds from the north may indicate cold air is arriving, while winds from the south may indicate warm air. Additionally, wind direction can affect temperature, humidity, and cloud formation.
- Observe changes in wind direction: A change in wind direction can indicate a change in weather conditions. For example, a wind passing from south to north may indicate the arrival of a cold front, while a wind passing from north to south may indicate the arrival of a warm front.
- Observe warm or cold wind: Warm or cold wind can indicate the origin of air masses and the type of climate. For example, a warm wind from a desert area may indicate an arid climate, while a cold wind from the North Pole may indicate a cold climate.

In addition, the wind can affect the choice of site for setting up camp, the choice of activities to be carried out and the safety of the outdoor activity. For example, a strong wind can make shelter construction or food preparation difficult, while a weak wind can favor the use of fire for heating and cooking.

Understanding climate based on plants is an important skill for bushcrafters. Plants can provide valuable insights into the local climate, soil conditions and water levels in each area.

Here are some tips for understanding climate based on plants:

- Observe the plant species present: the plants present in a given area can indicate the type of climate, the availability of water and the conditions of the soil. For example, the presence of plants that need a lot of water can indicate the presence of a humid climate, while the presence of drought-tolerant plants can indicate an arid climate.
- Observing plant blooms: Plant blooms can provide insight into the season and weather conditions. For example, early flowering may indicate a mild winter, while late flowering may indicate a cold winter.
- Observe plant shape and density: Plant shape and density can indicate the type of climate and soil conditions. For example, plants with large, thin leaves may indicate a humid climate, while plants with small, thick leaves may indicate an arid climate.
- Observe the color of the leaves: The color of the leaves can indicate the health of the plants and the condition of the soil. For example, yellow or brown leaves can indicate nutrient-poor soil or water scarcity.

In addition, plant knowledge can be useful in choosing materials for shelter construction and food preparation, researching medicinal herbs, and evaluating food safety. However, it's important to note that understanding climate based on plants takes practice and experience.

Trees, too, can provide valuable insights into local weather conditions, seasons, and wind direction. Here are some tips for understanding the weather based on trees:

- Observe wind direction: Trees can give indications of wind direction, especially taller trees.
- Observe the shape of trees: The shape of trees can indicate local weather conditions. For example, trees with branches that lean upwards may indicate strong and persistent winds, while trees with branches that hang downwards may indicate humid weather.
- Observing leaf fall: Leaf fall can indicate the season and weather conditions. For example, early leaf fall may indicate a cold autumn, while late leaf fall may indicate a mild autumn.
- Observe the humidity in the air: trees can provide information on the humidity in the air. For example, the presence of condensation on the leaves can indicate high air humidity.

Another way to understand weather changes in nature is to observe the behavior of animals. Animals have developed natural abilities to adapt to their environment and weather conditions and can provide insight into current conditions.

Here are some examples of how animals can provide information about weather conditions:

- Birds: Birds can indicate the presence of adverse weather conditions. For example, seagulls may fly higher than usual before a storm, while blackbirds may sing more before a sunny day.

- Ants: Ants can indicate the arrival of an imminent rain. When ants are moving quickly and congregating in large groups, it can indicate that rain is impending.
- Hamsters: Hamsters can provide information about outside temperatures. When hamsters build nests deeper than usual, it can indicate that the weather is getting colder.
- Crickets: Crickets can provide information about night-time temperatures. When crickets are chirping louder than usual, it can indicate that the nighttime temperature is warm and stable.

A final way to understand the weather is by reading the clouds. Clouds can provide valuable information about the current weather situation and its short-term evolution.

Here are some examples of how clouds can provide information about weather conditions:

- Low, dark clouds: Low, dark clouds, such as rain clouds or storm clouds, can indicate that severe weather is on the way.
- High, thin clouds: High, thin clouds, such as cirrus clouds, can indicate a change in weather conditions. For example, the appearance of cirrus clouds can indicate the arrival of an impending storm.
- Cumulus Clouds: Cumulus clouds, such as cumulonimbus clouds, can indicate thunderstorms or showers. These clouds have an upright shape and develop rapidly.
- Clouds with a colored halo: Clouds with a colored halo, such as nacre clouds, can indicate that the weather is changing. These clouds form at high altitudes and are often associated with high winds or an oncoming storm.

How to prepare for different weather conditions

Thunderstorms and lightning represent one of the greatest dangers for those who venture into nature and are often greatly underestimated.

Unfortunately, however, every year they claim dozens of victims especially in summer when the atmospheric phenomenon is more frequent.

How should we behave if we are suddenly caught by a storm? The first thing is to understand the clues that herald the arrival of storms and lightning. The most common signs are:

- Feel a slight tickling sensation in the parts where the skin is exposed.
- Similar sensation also on the scalp and the hair stands on end.
- You may hear a buzzing sound and a soft sound from metal objects.
- You can spot blue flames called Saint Elmo's fires in correspondence with particularly exposed metal objects such as summit crosses or poles.

The approximate distance of a thunderstorm in kilometers can be calculated by dividing the number of seconds between lightning and sound by three.

Example: If the time interval between lightning and thunder is ten seconds, the center of the storm is only two miles away. So, the time has come to take appropriate protective measures.

How to behave in case of lightning and thunderstorms in nature?

- Avoid ridges, isolated rock formations and keep at least 15 meters away from them.
- All metal parts of your equipment must stay away from you.
- Avoid taking cover in gullies, crevices, chimneys, hollows, caves (if they are not very deep), large, isolated boulders and trees.
- It is safer to position yourself on snowy terrain or glaciers rather than rocky terrain.
- Avoid gatherings of people or animals.
- Don't stand, and don't walk. Get into a crouched position with feet together and knees drawn up against your chest while sitting on your pack.

How to deal with the rain

Let's start by saying that even if the temperatures are around 10/12 °C, choosing to get wet to dry off later is not a wise choice, a wet body at those temperatures cools down very quickly and the risk of thermal stress is very high. If the temperatures, on the other hand, are around 16/18 °C, you can easily choose to get wet and then dry off later.

Rain and wind together are excellent allies to lower body temperature suddenly, don't choose to face them both. If you decide to get wet, do it only if you have a dry change in your bag with you or you will regret it bitterly.

If you choose to stay in the rain, do so only if you don't use clothing that tends to get soaked quickly.

Don't stay wet for a long time and don't fall asleep with wet clothes on, temperatures drop rapidly at night.

If you've gotten wet and don't have gear with you, it's wise to light a fire (as soon as possible) to dry your clothes while running out of clothing. The fire will also warm you and dry your clothes quickly.

Dealing with extreme weather conditions

Bushcraft involves the ability to adapt to natural conditions, including changes in the weather. However, in some situations, weather conditions can become extreme and pose a safety hazard.

How to deal with blizzards

Blizzards can present a very difficult challenge to deal with while bushcrafting, but there are certain techniques that can help prevent danger and ensure survival in these extreme weather conditions. Here are some tips on how to deal with blizzards while bushcrafting:

- Use natural thermal insulators. The right clothing can make a big difference in the outdoors, not only for comfort but for survival itself. When the weather turns unexpectedly bad, like in the case of blizzards, and your clothing isn't protective enough, fall back on one of the oldest survival tricks: create natural padding, using the insulation that plants can provide. Live or dead plants, can be tucked into pant legs and between layers of clothing, so they aren't in direct contact with the skin. Of course, you will feel unclean and perhaps in the company of some ants, but the layer of air that will remain trapped inside the leaves will allow you to feel less cold and perhaps avoid hypothermia.
- Build a Shelter: Building a proper shelter can provide some protection from snow and wind. The shelter should be constructed of wind and snow resistant materials and should be in an elevated, non-floodable area.
- Build a Snow Barrier: If you are forced to be outdoors during a snowstorm, you can build a snow barrier around your body to protect yourself from the wind.

Hurricanes

Dealing with a hurricane while bushcrafting can be extremely dangerous and requires a great deal of preparation. Here are some tips on dealing with hurricanes while bushcrafting:

- Stay informed: Following the weather forecast and warnings from local authorities is vital to avoid being trapped in a dangerous area.
- Finding Safe Shelter: Look for a safe shelter, such as a solid building or cave, to protect yourself from wind and rain. If you cannot find a safe shelter, look for an area protected from sea waves and build a wind resistant shelter.
- Take the necessary precautions: make sure you have clothing suitable for the cold and humidity, food, drinking water and equipment to start a fire.
- Avoid Trees: Avoid approaching trees, as strong gusts of wind can knock them down and pose a mortal danger.

Floods

Floods are another rather frequent and common risk, especially in some areas. These too are often predictable, but not always.

The water level, in the event of a flood, can reach several meters and can even do so in a matter of minutes. Therefore, it is one of those eventualities for which it is good to be prepared, especially if you are exploring an area where the risk is present and, perhaps, has already occurred in the past. The first thing to do in the event of a flood is to leave everything and move as far away as possible from the area where the flooding is taking place. Seek refuge in high places, such as climbing a tree. Avoid taking refuge in closed places such as caves or seeking refuge under bridges or other areas where water flows. Once the flood is over, always try to pay attention to the areas where the water has receded, it could be completely muddy, and you could get trapped.

Chapter 2: Naturalist Skills and Environmental Awareness

The importance of understanding and appreciating nature in bushcraft

For us humans, nature is invaluable. We still cannot live without nature. In fact, we may depend more than ever on healthy and resilient ecosystems to ensure the long-term well-being of an (ever) increasing number of citizens around the world.

Our atmosphere, forests, rivers, oceans and soils continue to provide us with the air we breathe, the food we eat, the water we drink and the raw materials we consume, as well as spaces for recreation and refreshment.

But the value of nature exceeds the direct services it provides us. Nature also has a cultural value, because it serves as the background of our existence as human beings and provides us with the necessary conditions to allow us to enjoy good physical and mental health, as well as to find emotional and spiritual well-being.

Nature has an intrinsic value, in which human beings are involved in the limited role of custodians, with an ethical responsibility towards nature itself, our society and above all that of future generations.

However, we tend to take nature for granted, considering it as a "free" resource to draw on not only for our needs, but also for our desires. This behavior justifies more than ever the importance of understanding and recognizing the true value of nature.

Understanding and appreciating nature is central to bushcrafting. Understanding nature helps to prevent dangerous situations and to react promptly in an emergency. For example, knowledge about toxic plants or weather conditions can help you avoid problems and maintain personal safety.

Understanding the natural resources available and how to use them effectively can help you survive in emergency situations. Learning to find food, water, shelter and how to make a fire are essential skills for survival in the wild.

Nature can be of enormous physical but also mental benefit. Being immersed in nature can reduce stress and promote concentration. Furthermore, physical activity and contact with nature are beneficial for health.

In summary, an understanding and appreciation of nature is fundamental to the practice of bushcraft, which is based on the knowledge and use of natural resources for survival and well-being in a wild and untouched environment.

Basic ecology

Ecology is a science that studies the interactions and relationships between living organisms and their environment. These studies include other living organisms, abiotic factors such as climate, geology, and soil, as well as human activities. It examines how organisms interact with each other and their environment to form ecosystems and how those ecosystems change over time.

Ecology is not limited to studying the environment and the Earth alone. It is a multidisciplinary field that integrates knowledge from biology, geology, chemistry, physics, mathematics, and social sciences to understand how living organisms and their environment interact and how these interactions can be sustained for the benefit of both present and future generations.

It is therefore a discipline that studies the various living systems that occupy the same territory, interacting with it on the basis of various factors (physical, geographical, chemical).

In practice, ecology understands and clarifies the mechanisms that regulate natural balances. In doing so, it is possible to intervene on these balances to avoid, for example, the extinction of species, both animal and vegetable, as well as guaranteeing their use on the basis of the principle of sustainable development.

To have a general knowledge of ecological functioning, it is necessary to know:

- The hierarchy of ecological organization
- The mechanisms underlying the principle of biodiversity.
- The relationships between species and organisms, as well as the structure and functioning of communities.

All these principles are fundamental for safeguarding the environment and, consequently, also safeguarding human health and psycho-physical well-being.

What is meant by ecosystem?

It is a system made up of 2 elements that are joined together in a very close relationship: living organisms and the physical environment in which they live.

There are several ecosystems, each of which is made up of one (or more) community of living organisms and also of non-living elements that have various types of interactions with each other.

Ecosystems have 4 peculiarities:

- These are open systems.
- They are always composed of a biotic component (animal and plant living beings that can be primary producers, consumers and decomposers) and an abiotic one (non-living organisms, organic and inorganic components).
- They tend to reach, and then maintain, a certain evolutionary stability, or a dynamic equilibrium.
- They are interconnected with other ecosystems; together they form macro-ecosystems that are defined as landscapes.

It is possible to distinguish 2 types of ecosystems:

- Natural: they are those which, once the ecological balance has been reached, have a high gross productivity and zero net productivity.
- Artificial: with lower gross productivity and positive (agricultural) or negative (urban) net productivity.

There are two classes of ecosystems:

Generalized, which includes a vast and varied complexity of animal and plant species that live together in a symbiotic way and whose imbalance can generate chain consequences, even quite serious.

Specialized: type of ecosystem that produces a lot but, at the same time, impoverishes the earth.

What is biodiversity? The concept of biodiversity is closely related to the concept of ecosystem.

When an ecosystem is fragile we say that it has a low level of biodiversity. It is essential to safeguard the biodiversity of an ecosystem as biodiversity itself represents the variety of living beings, their habitats and the ecosystems related to them.

Losing biodiversity means altering ecosystem processes so much as to put the ecosystem itself and the services it provides to man at risk.

What does ecology do? Analyze and study the interactions between living beings and the environment in which they live. Here is specifically what those involved in ecology do:

- It catalogs data on the various species present in a certain natural environment, on the number of individuals belonging to these species as well as on the relationships that the various species establish among themselves.
- Reconstructs the environments to be studied in the laboratory.
- Develops mathematical models through which to describe the various interactions detected in each ecosystem.

By studying the interactions that link living beings to the environment in which they live, ecology makes it possible to predict how these beings could behave in the face of any changes. All of humanity depends on the natural environment for many things: water, food, climate, health.

Nowadays we are witnessing a double combination of factors: the increasingly rapid growth of the human population on the one hand and the continuous deterioration of the natural environments presents on Earth on the other.

Knowing the laws of ecology therefore becomes essential above all because it gives us the possibility of being able to intervene to restore the balance that has been lost.

Wildlife identification and behavior

Wildlife identification and behavior are important skills for bushcrafting. Here are some helpful tips:
- Study animal recognition guides: There are many guides available that help identify animals in the wild, with pictures and detailed descriptions.

- Look closely: To identify animals, it's important to look closely at their appearance, behavior, and habitat. For example, the appearance and size of the body, the type of fur, the shape of the beak or the legs can be useful indicators for the identification of different species.
- Know the habits of animals: each animal has a specific behavior that depends on its survival needs, the seasons and the territory in which it lives. Knowing these habits can help predict their movement and behavior.
- Keep your distance: When observing wildlife, it is important to keep a safe distance to avoid scaring them or putting yourself in danger. Also, you should never go near wild animals or attempt to touch them.
- Respect animals: wild animals are an important part of the ecosystem and deserve respect. You should never disturb them, hunt them illegally or damage their habitat.

Having said that, let's go into a little more detail. Know that in nature you will find many dangerous wild animals and for which you must never let your guard down. After all, the forest is their habitat, therefore we cannot be caught off guard and accuse the specimens of having attacked us, if we ourselves have not been able to respect the basic rules to prevent an attack or a clash. So let's see which animals are not to be underestimated and how to behave if you encounter them.

Wolf

The wolf is an animal that lives in our mountain ranges and which, like all wild animals, has distrust of man. He therefore has no interest in attacking hikers who cross his path, but duly keeps away from them. His extremely developed senses, in fact, allow him to understand the presence of man before the latter has time to realize it.

However, there are some circumstances under which the wolf could feel threatened, and assume an aggressive attitude. One of these is the moment of the meal: all the animals feel particularly defenseless while they are feeding; therefore, it is advisable not to approach the specimen intent on eating, but to move away cautiously without giving the impression of posing a threat to the wolf.

The presence of puppies is one of the circumstances that can push the wolf to simulate an attack, precisely to defend them: it is a "false" threat, made up of howls and growls, aimed at frightening the hiker and making him move away from his den. In this case, as in the event of an encounter with a wounded specimen, the tactic to get out unharmed is to move away without ever turning your back on the animal, but always keeping your gaze fixed on it without making sudden or unexpected movements. During excursions in areas notoriously populated by wolves, the advice is to always keep the dogs under close supervision: these animals tend to annoy the wolves a lot, who will feel the instinct to attack by taking over the dog and sometimes even the owner who holds on a leash or in her arms.

In the unfortunate event of being surrounded by a pack of wolves, always keep your face turned towards them and assume an aggressive attitude with clapping and shouting, to scare them. Always avoid running away and turning your back on animals.

Bear

The majestic bear is not difficult to meet in high mountain landscapes, especially during the summer season. This solitary animal has no interest in attacking humans, unless it feels directly threatened, as in the case it is surprised during a meal, or in the presence of its own litter. The advice is to keep at least 100 m away from the bear, and to limit yourself to observing it without trying to get closer.

Should you find yourself in close contact with a bear and its cubs, it is good to keep in mind that this animal is capable of climbing trees and tends to stand up on two feet not so much to attack as to focus on the situation in which it is finding. The important thing is not to scream or make sudden movements, but to speak normally so that the animal can identify us and not mistake us for a threat. In most cases, the bear will tend to simulate an attack with the aim of frightening us and making us move away from its territory and its den.

In the unfortunate event he should really seek physical confrontation, the directive of the experts is to lie down on the ground with his face turned towards the ground, covering his neck with his hands for protection, without moving. Attempting to defend yourself with any movement would not lead to success, while remaining motionless will make the mammal understand that it poses no threat.

To keep bears away as much as possible and avoid this type of encounter, it is advisable to properly clean the rest areas and not leave food scraps within the reach of the animals. In addition, lighting a bonfire can be a very useful solution to keep not only bears but also other possible threats away from the woods.

Wild boars

The wild boar is one of the easiest animals to meet during a hike. Also in this case, the animal by itself has no interest in interacting and even less in attacking humans, except in the case of very specific situations.

If the boar were to be caught off guard and find himself with no way out, his instinct could lead him to attack precisely because he was extremely afraid. The same thing could happen to a female specimen in the company of her puppies: to bring them to safety she would be willing to do anything, including attacking the unfortunate hiker.

It is therefore advisable to always make discreet noise during your walks, so that the animals sense your presence in advance and are careful not to approach you, running into unpleasant situations for both parties.

Furthermore, it is advisable to always clean the rest areas adequately, not leaving food and rubbish residues within the reach of wild boars and other species, which could approach you driven by curiosity. If you find yourself at very close range with a wild boar, it is recommended that you move away with caution, without making sudden noises, and without ever turning your back on it.

Ticks

Speaking of small animals, we cannot fail to dwell on the much-hated ticks. These tiny parasites are carriers of serious pathologies such as Lyme disease, which develops months and sometimes years after the original bite, causing joint problems and permanent damage to the cardiac and neurological system. Ticks usually live clinging to wild mammals such as mice, squirrels, deer, wild boars, but they can also attack humans without problems. Being hematophagous, these parasites feed on the blood of the host subject, which leads them to swell and even reach 1cm in diameter. If on an "empty stomach" they are difficult to identify, after having eaten they are much easier to find and remove.

Preferring areas with low and sparse grass for camping is a very wise choice, compared to areas where the vegetation is dense and the air is very humid, such as for example near ponds and watercourses: this is where ticks tend to proliferate.

To avoid ticks, technical clothing is recommended, with long trousers and high socks at least up to the calf. It is also essential to use a specific spray against ticks, which protects against bites for the entire duration of the excursion.

Venomous snakes

If you spot a venomous snake while bushcrafting, it's important to stay calm and take a few precautions. The first thing to do is keep your distance. Venomous snakes are usually shy and try to avoid humans; therefore, if possible, keep a distance of at least 2-3 meters from the snake and do not try to get close to it.

Try to identify the species of snake you have encountered. This can help determine whether or not it is poisonous, as well as assess the risk to you and other members of your party.

Don't try to touch the snake, even with a stick or other equipment. This could cause the snake to react aggressively.

Don't try to drive the snake away by force or by using chemicals, such as insect repellents. This could make the snake angry and lead to a seizure.

Wait for the snake to leave. Typically, venomous snakes try to avoid humans and if they feel threatened, they slowly drift away. If you're in an open area, wait for the snake to slowly walk away.

There are also ways to prevent venomous snake bites. First is the choice of the right clothing, consisting of thick and high socks, long and not too thin trousers and above all ankle boots, which cover the sensitive area and make a possible bite more unlikely.

Secondly, when you decide to camp for a break, it is always advisable to light a fire to keep unwanted and potentially dangerous animals away. Choosing your bed carefully can save us from unpleasant inconveniences: it is always better to stay away from waterways and wetlands but prefer the hinterland and possibly clearings where there are not too many bushes or shrubs.

Last, but not least, we mention the use of a hiking stick, very useful for testing the surrounding terrain before putting your feet on it, and for chasing away snakes even before they can perceive us as a danger and go on the attack. Even when harvesting fruits and branches, we always recommend paying close attention, and possibly pushing all the leaves away with the stick before bringing your hands to the ground.

Ethical considerations in bushcraft

Bushcraft is a practice that requires a deep understanding and respect for nature and the surrounding environment. Therefore, there are some ethical considerations that bushcraft practitioners should keep in mind:

- Respect for nature: bushcraft is a practice based on the use of natural resources. It is important that bushcraft practitioners be respectful of the environment and surrounding flora and fauna. One should try to minimize the impact on the surrounding environment and use only the resources necessary for survival.
- Knowledge and compliance with local laws: Bushcraft practitioners should be aware of local laws and comply with regulations regarding the use of natural resources. This may include restrictions on collecting firewood or hunting certain species of animals.
- Rejection of excess: Bushcraft should be practiced sustainably and responsibly. This means that practitioners should avoid waste and excessive use of natural resources. One should try to use only what is necessary for survival and not waste resources.
- Rejection of the use of harmful chemicals: Bushcraft should be practiced using only natural and sustainable techniques. This means that practitioners should avoid using harmful chemicals that can harm their surroundings.

How to develop a connection to the natural

The implications that nature has on our health, including psychological ones, are much more than we imagine.

According to tribal philosophy, every plant, hill, mountain, stone that was on the Earth before the coming of man emanates a subtle energy that has healing powers. Whether we are aware of it or not, there are all the necessary elements and principles in nature for healing.

Mother nature not only gives us oxygen to keep us alive, the food we eat, the flowers to adorn our homes, the water to quench our thirst and wash ourselves but it is a continuous source of energy and serenity.

According to recent studies, the connection with nature is associated with greater:

- Autonomy
- Self-esteem
- Sense of purpose in life
- Attention span
- Anxiety
- Depression
- Stress.

In recent years there has been a growing interest in the relationship between nature and public health. Numerous scientific studies have shown that spending time outdoors and in contact with nature can have positive effects on people's physical and mental health.

Healthcare professionals are increasingly using nature as a tool to promote a healthy lifestyle and improve patient health. For example, many hospitals are creating therapeutic gardens, green spaces where patients can spend time outdoors and relax during their healing journey.

Additionally, some doctors are prescribing "doses of nature" to their patients, encouraging them to spend time outdoors and in contact with nature as part of their medical treatment. This can include activities like walking in the park, hiking in the mountains, or even just spending time in a garden.

Connecting with nature can have a positive impact not only on people's health, but also on the wider natural environment. People who spend time outdoors and develop a greater awareness and appreciation for nature tend to become more sensitive to environmental issues and adopt more environmentally sustainable behaviors.

For example, people who spend time in nature can become more aware of the impact of their actions on the environment and therefore adopt more sustainable behaviors such as recycling, using eco-friendly means of transport, reducing energy and the adoption of sustainable agricultural practices.

Furthermore, people who feel connected to nature are more inclined to support policies and initiatives for nature conservation and environmental protection, thus becoming true ambassadors of the natural environment.

At a time when the world is confronted with growing environmental threats such as climate change, biodiversity loss and ecosystem degradation, understanding and strengthening the connection between people and nature is essential to promote initiatives that favor the conservation of environment.

A greater connection with nature can in fact lead people to develop a sense of responsibility and care for the natural environment. When people feel part of nature and appreciate its beauty and its importance to human well-being, they are more inclined to engage in its conservation and protection. There are many initiatives that can be promoted to strengthen the connection between people and nature, for example the creation of urban parks, community gardens and environmental education programs involving schools and civil society.

Furthermore, it is important to promote policies and initiatives that favor the conservation and protection of the environment, for example through the protection of protected areas, the reduction of greenhouse gas emissions and the promotion of renewable energy sources.

In conclusion, understanding and strengthening the connection between people and nature is essential to stimulate initiatives that favor environmental protection and the creation of a more sustainable and resilient society.

PART 8: COMPLETE LIST OF MOST IMPORTANT EQUIPMENTS AND TOOLS

In bushcraft, the right equipment is essential for survival and comfort in the wild. Without the right equipment, bushcraft activities can become very difficult or even impossible to carry out.

For example, a good tent or makeshift shelter can provide shelter from water, wind and insects. A good source of fire is essential for cooking, heating and purifying water. A durable and versatile knife is essential equipment for food preparation, shelter construction, and woodworking. A compass or GPS are essential for orienting and moving safely in the natural environment.

Even if you have the best equipment, if you don't know how to use it properly or don't have the basic skills to survive in the natural environment, you may find yourself in trouble.

In this book you will be provided with a list of all the essential equipment to be able to live peacefully in nature.

Bushcraft backpacks and bags

Having a survival kit can make the bushcraft experience easier to manage, but to carry all the items you need to have a backpack or bag that can contain them and make them available when needed. There are many bags on the market designed for bushcraft. But for what reasons do these accessories differ from the others in common use?

Bushcraft backpacks are designed to be easily transportable, but at the same time they must guarantee excellent resistance. Bumps and unexpected events are always around the corner! Usually, these models are equipped with many pockets. Each of them is used for a precise task, without creating confusion. Thus, even in the most critical moments, you will always know exactly where a particular object is kept. Bushcraft bags vary in materials, sizes and the purpose for which they are made; there are some backpacks with a maximum capacity of 30 liters, while some bags tolerate more than 50 liters. These accessories are made so that the weight is distributed over the whole body and not just on the back, and they can have an internal frame that allows you to adjust the load.

Bushcraft clothing, shirts and trousers

Clothing is connected to the climate of the place you choose to visit. There are no specific rules in this sector, but the important thing is to opt for clothing that is sturdy, comfortable and that can best protect every part of the body. If you choose a cold place, layered clothing is recommended, to regulate body temperature and not disperse heat.

Here is a small diagram for reference:

- Undergarments: Seamless and elastic knickers and undershirts
- Thermal trousers and shirts: insulate from the cold and prevent phenomena such as perspiration.
- Sweaters, sweatshirts, trousers, fleeces, jackets: they form an additional thermal barrier.
- Jackets, over trousers, capes: they protect against atmospheric agents such as wind and rain.
- Gloves, double or thick socks, hats, visors, earmuffs, neck warmers: they offer the ultimate level of protection, going to repair the extremities of the body which are more vulnerable to the cold.
- High boots: protect from cold and foreign bodies.
- In summer and in hot places it is necessary to wear clothing that can protect you from the sun and insects, and footwear that protects the foot.

Survival equipment and accessories

If you can't wait to leave and experience these fantastic sensations on your skin, remember to bring your kit of survival equipment and accessories with you. The essential objects for your survival and which you will not be able to do without in any case are:
- A fixed blade knife with case
- Tent (or alternatively a tarp)
- Sleeping bag or thermal blanket
- Torch
- Rope
- Lighter or matches
- First aid kit
- Saw or cutter.

Water bag for bushcraft

Water supplies are the first thing to consider when preparing to organize a bushcrafting excursion. Indeed, finding it in nature may not be immediate and may take some time; therefore, it is always better to go out properly equipped. The most important thing is to have a comfortable and light container for liquids: for this there are practical and eco-friendly water bags.

Carrying a now obsolete plastic bottle with you is certainly not in the true bushcrafter's pocket, above all because it is the most harmful container for the environment, less hygienic and less durable over time. A worthy substitute is certainly the water bottle, or even the filter straw.

The water bag, or hydration bag, on the other hand, is made of soft plastic material with a tube that comes out of one end and turns into a real straw to draw from. The mouth of the straw is always equipped with a valve that closes when it stops sucking in water, so as not to cause unnecessary waste of such a precious commodity, especially during a bushcrafting excursion.

The water bag therefore constitutes an immediate and easy access to the water reserve, especially during the most difficult situations or rough paths. Placed in the backpack, it is always available and ready to dispense, it does not require the use of the hands and therefore allows you to drink even when you are busy doing something else, without having to stop to take the water out of the backpack and then put it away.

It is an eco-friendly solution precisely because, given its nature, it is very unlikely that it will be forgotten along the path to pollute the environment, as happens too often with plastic bottles.

The capacity of the water bags varies according to the models and can range from approximately 1L to 3L. When choosing yours, it is good to consider all factors, such as ease of cleaning, ease of filling and whether it is resistant to sudden changes in temperature. In fact, many bags contain an insulating bladder inside them which prevents the water from freezing in extreme cold conditions, but also from becoming boiling hot in the middle of summer.

Tarp: the waterproof bushcraft tarp

When we talk about tarp, we want to refer to a very simple sheet that can provide excellent shelter to those who choose it as their personal shelter. Unlike tents, it is lighter and therefore much easier to transport, and can be used as an emergency shelter or as a source of shelter from rain and wind.

It is a valid alternative to the classic survival tent, and certainly choosing it will result in considerable savings. Not to mention the advantage offered by the reduction of the formation of condensation and the possibility of choosing it in different sizes.

Surely it is an aid that cannot be missing in the bushcraft equipment of a professional, as in many situations its presence proves to be truly fundamental. Before buying a bushcraft tarp you need to evaluate its measurements and dimensions, the presence of anchor points and the weight of the structure, not forgetting to study the best configuration.

Here is a small ranking of the best tarps that exist on the market:

- Qeedo Smart Tarp. Tarp available in different sizes including the 3×3, the most requested in this sector. It is a high-quality towel with a simple and functional design. It can be used in various ways, both in the trekking and in the bushcraft sector, proving to be very useful especially in case of emergency. Thanks to the aluminum pegs it will be very easy to anchor to the ground, as they will not yield even after very strong tensions. It is a very popular model and turns out to be an excellent purchase in terms of quality and price.
- Anyoo camping towel. Very valid tarp if used for excursions or outdoor trips, as it is able to offer a lot of protection both from the sun's rays and from the rain, wind and snow. It can be connected to the trees via ropes or be supported by the presence of the supplied poles which will allow you to fix it accurately and safely. Thanks to its size it will be very comfortable to use, and the fabric will guarantee excellent performance regardless of the climate and context of use. The model in question

is also very compact and very light, an element to be appreciated especially in the case of large excursions on foot. Obviously, you have to take care of it and pay attention to the components, which could be damaged if they were treated with negligence.

- Tarp Bushmen Thermo Tarp 3×3. Very sought after tarp, which unlike the other models mentioned above exploits the thermal component which makes a complete tarp. The model described is a breathable, waterproof and insulating tarp, after which, thanks to the silver coating, it is able to reflect the sun's rays, reducing the accumulation of heat. An advantage of this model is that it can be used as a rescue blanket in the event of hypothermia, as it could insulate the body of the affected person by offering them the heat useful for survival until help arrives. The only flaw is that the seams can sometimes appear too coarse and easily damaged, even if with a little attention you can avoid any unforeseen events.
- DD Tarp XL Hammocks. Large tarp, designed to protect and shelter families and any pets. The material is very light but despite this it does not lack in terms of quality and resistance, as it proves to be able to support and provide the protections required by bushcraft. It belongs to the mid-range sheets and is highly appreciated by all buyers who have invested in this innovative product.
- Tarp As Amazonas Adventure Wing. Quite expensive upper-end tarp, but it will certainly not disappoint the expectations of those who decide to buy it. This sheet is designed to protect campers from atmospheric precipitation of all kinds, and if necessary, it can become a comfortable hammock where you can take a regenerating nap. It is a very light prototype that lends itself well to any situation, and thanks to the pegs and various anchor hooks it will be very stable once assembled. It is recommended for those who love nature and often set out for new exciting and suggestive experiences.

Bushcraft hammock

The hammock is not just a relaxing bed where you can read and swing but a tactical shelter where you can isolate yourself even in the most extreme conditions.

Many bushcrafters choose a practical tent as a shelter, or a TARP, or the multipurpose waterproof sheet. A technical hammock can be a very valid alternative to these two products: it is in fact very useful for avoiding animal attacks, for resting safely in the dense forest or for avoiding contact with the humidity with which, lying down on the ground, it is inevitable to have do.

The bushcrafting hammock is certainly not an accessory for everyone: sleeping a whole night hanging and swinging may not be ideal for some hikers, who prefer to keep their feet on the ground especially when, in a state of sleep or half asleep, it is not possible keep control of the situation.

As it is logical to understand, the bushcraft hammock is made of very different materials from the domestic one and must respect some precise characteristics to be considered suitable for use of this type. First of all, it must be ultra-light and perfect for transport: the bushcrafter must be able to keep everything he needs inside his backpack to spend days and days in unspoiled nature. Each tool and accessory must have optimized dimensions and weight, be neither bulky nor heavy to carry on the shoulders. The technical hammock usually weighs less than 35 oz, including its hooks. It must then be easy to fix: nowadays everything is focused on ease of use and practicality of assembly, and the bushcrafting hammock certainly cannot be outdone. It must therefore be inexperienced-proof, and be able to be fixed in record time, guaranteeing stability and safety.

The material used to make the hammock is imperatively waterproof, to resist any showers, humidity in the area, and any inconvenience that may occur during its use. Usually, the technical hammock is designed to support one person at a time, but the most recent ones support such a heavy weight that they are also suitable for the use of two hikers at a time; however, this feature strictly depends on the manufacturer and model, and it is very important to check it before using it.

Last, but not least, is the mosquito net protection on the top of the hammock, which shelters the hiker from potentially dangerous animals and insects that swarm in the wooded areas and dense vegetation. Many hammocks also have compartments and pockets to be able to comfortably store your belongings during your rest hours, without fear of them being lost. There is also the possibility of equipping yourself with special sleeping bags for hammocks, to take advantage of this tactical shelter even in the coldest periods or places.

Water bottle with mess tin

The water bottle with integrated mess tin is convenient for drinking and cooking, saving a lot of space and additional weight compared to those who carry an entire mess tin with various pots and separate water bottles.

Titanium water bottles are the best even if unfortunately, very expensive. Titanium is an element that makes them very light, highly resistant, non-toxic to humans and anti-corrosive. They cost a lot, but they have to be taken into account if we want a definitive bottle that will accompany us throughout our life during our adventures.

Head Torch

The head torch is a portable lighting device that is worn on the head thanks to an elastic band. This type of flashlight is especially useful during outdoor activities such as bushcraft, as it allows you to keep your hands free while lighting the road ahead.

In bushcraft, the headlamp is especially useful during night-time activities such as building shelters, gathering wood, preparing food, and navigating dimly lit areas. Thanks to its convenience, the head torch allows you to use both hands to perform the necessary tasks, without having to hold a traditional torch or lantern in your hand.

Furthermore, the front torch can also be used in emergency situations, such as searching for a campsite or a path during the night or in the event of a sudden blackout, allowing you to move around safely even in poor visibility conditions.

Sleeping bag

The sleeping bag is one of the essential materials for bushcraft and is mainly used as a shelter system from the cold and bad weather when sleeping outdoors.

During bushcraft activities, the night is often spent in a tent, under a natural shelter or even outdoors. In these situations, the sleeping bag becomes a fundamental element to guarantee a comfortable and restful sleep, keeping the body temperature constant and protecting from humidity and wind.

The sleeping bag is made with insulating materials that retain the heat produced by the body and prevent heat dispersion towards the outside. Additionally, the sleeping bag can be fitted with a hood that wraps around the head and neck, helping to maintain body temperature.

The sleeping bag is available in different shapes, sizes and levels of thermal insulation, according to personal needs and the climatic conditions of the place where the bushcraft activity takes place. Some sleeping bags are designed for extreme temperatures, while others are lighter and more compact for ease of transport.

Made in the USA
Las Vegas, NV
19 October 2023